A D V A N C E   P R A I S E

*Faking Balance*

"From family puzzles, the joy of shiny, clean new cars that have no hope of staying that way, and the complicated social dynamics of middle school girls to the chaos of life as a working parent, the Mommy track, the strains of finding good child care and trying not to cry in unforgiving corporate America, Lela Davison's wonderful new book, *Faking Balance*, captures the madness of the work-life juggle with warmth, wit and poignancy. A very fun, and very human, read from an astute observer of modern life."

**Brigid Schulte**, author of the *New York Times* bestselling *Overwhelmed: Work, Love and Play when No One has the Time* and award-winning *Washington Post* staff writer

"I'm constantly impressed by Lela Davidson's ability to draw me in and make me laugh at everything from Botox to water births. As a fellow corporate refugee, home party survivor, and recovering clean-car-aholic, it's so comforting to read Lela's hilarious take on everyday suburban life and know I'm not alone. *Faking Balance* is laugh out loud funny and highly relatable. Thank God Lela Davidson is faking it like the rest of us, or we'd have to take her out back and beat her with a compression sock full of Chuck E. Cheese tokens."

**Leslie Marinelli**, CEO and Editor-in-Chief of InThePowderRoom.com

"*Faking Balance* helps smart women understand why they're still struggling to strike the elusive 'balance' in their lives. I found myself nodding in agreement, snorting out loud, and wanting to spend a girls' night out with Lela!"

**Hollee Schwartz Temple**, author of *Good Enough Is the New Perfect: Finding Happiness and Success in Modern Motherhood*

"There's still so much pressure for working moms to feel and look like we have it all figured out even though we're winging it every day. What we need most are warm, compassionate, non-judgmental friends who are 100 percent honest about the many challenges while also making us laugh. Lela Davidson offers us all of this with *Faking Balance*."

**Michelle Cove**, Executive Director of MEDIAGIRLS and author of *I Love Mondays: And other confessions from working moms*

"From our favorite funny lady who brought us *Blacklisted from the PTA* and *Who Peed on My Yoga Mat*, Lela Davidson's latest compilation of hilarious, poignant and real life stories is dedicated to the hard working mom who clutches a brief case and diaper bag while climbing the corporate ladder and the jungle gym and trying not to get the wind knocked out of her. *Faking Balance* is the best thing for working moms since happy hour—and you're all invited!"

**Ellie Grossman**, author of award-winning *Mishegas of Motherhood. Raising Children To Leave The Nest...As Long As They Come Home For Dinner*

# FAKING BALANCE
## ADVENTURES IN WORK AND LIFE

*Michelle, Thanks so much for your support!*

# FAKING BALANCE
## ADVENTURES IN WORK AND LIFE

*Lela Davidson*

# LELA DAVIDSON

Author of the award-winning collections
*Blacklisted from the PTA* and *Who Peed On My Yoga Mat?*

JUPITER PRESS

**Faking Balance: Adventures in Work and Life**
by Lela Davidson

ISBN: 978-1-942545-02-6

Library of Congress Control Number: 2015936736

Cover images: © Studio MARMILADE - Fotolia.com,
© Akulamatiau - Dreamstime.com

Author photo: Christy Schmid Photography

**Published by Jupiter Press**
imprint of Wyatt-MacKenzie

JUPITER PRESS

jupiterpress@wyattmackenzie.com

*For my parents, Lou Nicksic and Marilyn Levan, who always kept their balance, one way or another.*

～❀～

# Part 1

# Part 2

# Part 3

# PART 1

# Making Babies, the Sexy Way

☙

THE BABY MAKING STARTED one Saturday afternoon, sitting in our very cool Seattle condo, the one with the herbs growing on the tiny lanai and the Trader Joe's across the street. Within walking distance was the gym where I spent no less than six hours a week, amazingly good and affordable restaurants, killer views, concerts, and half a dozen coffee shops. My husband and I did whatever we wanted. At 27, I felt the pressure of my biological clock. No one in my mother's family had made it past twenty before popping out at least one offspring. My mother-in-law had started referring to our cat as her only grandchild—maybe because we kept the kitty's portrait in a gilded frame on the mantle of the flip-a-switch gas fireplace.

It was time.

Had there been a good movie playing that weekend, or a band we hadn't yet seen, or maybe a special on design-your-own burritos, we might have delayed our decision. Instead, on a rainy Saturday with nothing better to do, we decided to have a baby. Apparently, we were that bored. Who could blame us? We had spent endless days riding ferries and mountain bikes, while sipping coffee in every incarnation. We had enjoyed countless temperate evenings on the lawn under the Space Needle with those excessive burritos and craft beer. We had two jobs and one car. What more could we possibly need?

Once we had committed to the task, there was no retreat. We spent the first day of our journey engaged in light-hearted procreation banter and a few practice runs. The next day, we began preparing for our task in earnest, starting at the bookstore because this was long before Google. Try to imagine a time, less than twenty years ago, when every answer was not immediately accessible at your fingertips. In order to learn about a topic in depth, you had to go to a library or a bookstore. And, boy, did we learn that day.

"It says here there is only a 20% chance of getting pregnant each month," I told John.

Suddenly, all those years playing defense against the ever-persistent sperm brigade seemed a monumental wasted effort. According to the drawings and descriptions of the complex and interdependent biological processes involved, getting pregnant was nearly impossible.

I became a woman obsessed. Oh, yes, this was going to happen. I am nothing if not an achiever. After consulting a few more books and a few friends, I decided daily sex was the answer. Ten days in a row, to be precise. We would practice the rhythm method in reverse. Because one never knows exactly when an egg will drop, I was determined to provide all-day-every-day access to sperm, whenever my egg decided to descend. All I needed was a steady supply of sperm for a three-day window before and after the projected ovulation day. It's a common calculation.

I might have made a spreadsheet.

John and I had heard it could take several months after I stopped taking the pill for me to get pregnant. No worries. Our concentrated sex schedule would pay off sooner or later. Surprisingly, ten-day-in-a-row sex is not that fun. Maybe a sure thing kills a mood, or maybe we just weren't that good at it. Regardless, after the first few days, the magic was gone. Still, we'd committed to the process.

"Come on," I said to him on Night Eight. "It's go time." By that point, conception was a mission, lingerie and sweet words not required.

"Really?" He looked at me, at the bed, at my scrappy sweatpants. "Let's sit this one out."

Sit it out? Was he insane?

"You know the drill. Ten days in a row." I pulled back the sheet. "Do you want to have a baby or not?"

Suit up—or in this case, don't—or get out.

"So what if it's not this month?" he said.

Oh, no, buddy.

We had a system. We had a deadline. The project had become less about getting pregnant and more about accomplishing a goal.

"Listen," I said. "We can skip tonight if you want, but when your child one day comes complaining to you that he can't go out with his friends because he doesn't turn 21 until *next* month, well, that's on you."

I'm seductive like that.

And so it was done.

A few weeks later, on another rainy Saturday, I peed on a stick and got the blessed two lines. Just as I had planned.

# There's No Crying in Corporate America

☙

I WAS A SENIOR ANALYST in the Seattle office of Arthur Andersen when I got pregnant the first time. I was also working on an extended assignment in San Francisco. Absence, along with healthy doses of family pressure and boredom, had apparently made our hearts grow fonder for family. "Senior analyst" was the title that enabled the firm to justify an hourly rate of $175, but the position was just above entry-level and I was barely out of orientation when the home pregnancy test came back positive.

My boss smiled and made pleasant conversation about my impending bundle of joy.

"I didn't think we gave you time for that," he said in a tone I like to interpret as wholly wholesome and referring to my weekdays spent in another state. "Good for you."

He was kind, but clearly conflicted. As a good Mormon, he genuinely wished me well in starting a family. As a partner, he had to be grieving all the non-billable hours my new addition represented.

When I planned to get pregnant, I had exactly zero intention of leaving the glamour of data modeling to be at home with my child. A girl doesn't just throw away a prime cubicle spot and the chance to work 50 or 80 hours a week. She does not lightly abandon the opportunity to be responsible for Very Important Depositions with Very Cranky Attorneys, maybe one day, if she plays her ten-key right. This was 1997, and like most other women I knew, I planned to do it all. I had the skills to do it, too.

Systems are my drug.

In middle school, I created a wall-sized chart to track my chores. In high school, even as I blew off classes and occasionally ran with a questionable crowd, I kept an impeccable Trapper Keeper. In college, I was naturally drawn to accounting because, while many people believe accounting is about math, it is actually nothing but a series of rules. Learn them, apply them diligently, and you win accounting. Of course, there is much room for subjectivity in accounting, as Arthur Andersen would later spectacularly demonstrate through its association with Enron and ultimate demise, but I didn't know all that. The profession seemed then, in my naïveté, to be all black and white. The only pesky gray I saw came down in a constant drizzle outside the windows of the business school library where I worked the odd *and* even problems in the back of every accounting text. On my professors' recommendations, I took the intensive study course and passed all parts of the CPA exam before I graduated and started work, where they warned I would be perpetually distracted by the ever-present pressure of those billable hours.

Accounting had rules, as did the working environment.

You only got a job at a big firm if you had top grades and understood the social conventions of the world's most conservative profession. Once settled into my cubicle, I eagerly adhered to the protocols and various chains of command. That was how I would own this place. Clear out the corner office, Old White Guy; I was moving in.

Managing conflict is easy when roles are clearly defined. Before increasing amounts of estrogen and progesterone started reworking my chemistry, I might have questioned my superiors, but I never would have challenged them directly. Pregnancy changed me. I got a preview for how drastically I would be transformed when one of my managers crossed a line I didn't know I had drawn.

I was still in my first trimester when Mark and I started working on the San Francisco project. I had spent months at the client site, working through the processes and deliverables that our office had been brought in to manage. It's hard to say in retrospect whether it was the grind of the commute or the raging hormones or just Mark's generally annoying demeanor that set me off. It's fair to say that I might have been a tiny bit cranky. The flights up and down the West Coast had lost their appeal long before I started growing a tiny human inside my body. Now, on top of not sleeping in my own bed, I felt perpetually fat, tired, and ravenous.

Then Mark starting bossing me around.

Mark was a first-year manager, eager to prove his worth to the firm and secure his placement on the partner track. Like everyone else I worked with, Mark was very smart. But unlike the rest of us, who had been selected in no small part for our ability to develop rapport with others, Mark wasn't exactly skilled in the social realm. But the tension between us wasn't entirely his fault. I resented Mark's sudden involvement in the project I had been managing on my own. In the months I spent taking early Monday morning flights and making late Friday night returns, Mark had been working from the Seattle office, apparently not reading my notes. The project was going well—I had 175 binders to prove it.

Mark wanted to change everything. Naturally, I had some questions about those changes that I perceived could threaten everything I had set in motion, and consequently extend my weekly commutes down the coast. Instead of addressing my concerns and answering my questions, Mark started a war.

"It's not your job to ask questions," he said. "It's your job to answer them."

My heart raced, my skin flushed, and waves of those pregnancy hormones surged through my bloodstream. I had worked every extra practice problem. I had completed two internships and attended countless chicken dinners, "casual" mixers, and sporting events that were actually interviews. I had worn navy pantyhose, using the color of dependability to prove my dedication down to the ethical qualities of my stockings. And for what? To be told that I was not in a position to ask a question?

Not acceptable.

Clearly, what Mark found unacceptable were not the questions, but the questioning.

I seethed.

For a week, he and I did not speak. The frustration grew until it came out where I least expected.

I was sitting across from Phillip (not Phil), a San Francisco partner I barely knew. The afternoon sunlight streamed through the window, shining on the Lucite mementos of his many accomplishments. Not a hair on his local-news-anchor head was out of place, and his skin was freakishly tan. He had the casual air of a partner, all his climbing behind him. That's where I wanted to be. That goal was so far off. To get there, I'd have to learn how to take ridiculous amounts of pressure, and not just the pregnancy kind. This kid was seriously compromising my bladder.

I was relaxing in Phillip-not-Phil's office, taking a break and chatting, when he casually crossed his legs and leaned back in his chair.

"How are you?" he asked.

I burst into tears.

Not a slow trickle, a dainty leak, but a big, uncontrollable, mess of sobs and snot. Extremely unbecoming behavior for an up-and-comer.

*Oh my god, I'm crying. At work.*

Although not specifically designated in the annual evaluation or peer ranking process, emotional upheaval was not an indicator of partner-track readiness.

*I'm crying at work in front of a partner.*

*I'm crying at work in front of a partner, and it's not even my partner. It's Phillip-not-Phil, who is prettier than I am even before I started retaining disproportionately large amounts of water and aggression.*

I like to think I would have held it together in front of someone I knew better. No way would I have cried in front of Mark. If he'd been around that day, I might have thrown a binder across the room, but I would *not* have wept. Unfortunately, I wasn't sitting across from arrogant Mark, but sweet Phillip-not-Phil, and I succumbed to that feeling you get when a stranger is nice to you. I let it all go, squandering my reputation in a moment of weakness.

Then, just as suddenly as it had begun, the crying was over. I had purged myself, which left me feeling better. Phillip-not-Phil over there on the other side of the desk remained just as composed after my outburst as before. Perhaps he had accumulated enough experience with women—pregnant women, even—to understand that crying wasn't going to become a regular thing. That I would not gather all the junior staff for a meeting about the correct placement of Post-It notes only to dissolve into a messy lump of feelings. He may have known this, but I did not. All I knew was that I had done the one thing you do not ever do at work. To paraphrase the great Tom Hanks as Coach Dugan in *A League of Their Own*: There's no crying in Corporate America. There's no crying at work. Ever. Not even when all you want is your home and your husband and your Sour Patch Kids.

I detested being a cliché, the crying pregnant woman. It was all Mark's fault.

Upon our return to the Seattle office, the usual damp air was tinged with an icy edge. *Don't even look at me*, I thought. The tension built, this thick silence, until finally,

I had had enough. That morning, I put on my very best maternity power suit from A Pea in the Pod.

"It is *on*," I told my husband that morning, adding that I might not have a job at the end of the day. I'm good at drama when I want to be.

"You tell 'em, babe," he said.

Later that morning I walked into Mark's office and shut the door. "We have to talk."

*It's not me, it's you.*

"If you have a problem with me asking questions," I said, "I'm not sure we can work together."

Oh yeah, I was totally breaking up with my boss—and it felt fantastic.

Mark let me speak. The tension lifted. And then, just like my weepy moment with Phillip-not-Phil, it was over. But I was a changed woman, for the better.

Who could predict that a positive result on a pregnancy test would transform me from an ordinary accountant with good hair and a fledgling 401k into to a different organism entirely? I'd need that new fortitude to manage the rigors of being responsible for keeping another human alive. It takes a certain strength to ensure one's offspring do not grow up to kill puppies or star in porn. Or a reality show. You can't just leave a baby on the hood of the car or forget to water it for three weeks like that sad philodendron on the filing cabinet.

Those unstable pregnancy hormones prepare us for the coming onslaught of heightened emotions, including but not limited to, awe, wonder, love, empathy, angst, indecision, sadness, joy, confusion, and guilt to a previously unknown degree.

A few weeks later, I received my annual review. Phillip-not-Phil did not mention my minor breakdown, and Mark's contribution glowed with admiration. My altered emotional state hadn't been so damaging after all.

Even the rain didn't look so bad through the windows above my orderly laminate desk.

# Maternity Leave for Fun and Profit

࿔

DURING MY JUNIOR YEAR at the University of Washington, I did everything in my power to get a job at a Big Six firm. I participated in the accounting society, attended all the on- and off-campus recruiting events, and spent hours in the career counseling office reviewing tape and attempting to break myself of the eye-roll habit. A woman I knew from my hometown had such a job, so I invited her to lunch one day to get an insider's view. She gave me insight into the recruiting process.

"They need you more than you need them," she said. "You're the asset. Without you, they can't bill hours. Don't forget that."

The advice was no help at all to someone as intent to work in the most competitive part of the industry as I was, but it did help me to understand how the firms worked. They wanted you to want them. The more of us who wanted in, the better their pickings when it came time to fill the limited number of spots available. Arthur Andersen attracted me with their tradition and prestige. I didn't need a firm that catered to cool kids. I craved structure and status. Though the topic was covered, the ways in which my future employer treated women—mothers in particular—was of no concern to me. I lived in a bubble of innocence where glass ceilings were not glass at all, but rather unicorn glaze that I might tap through with nothing stronger than a single .5mm lead from my trusty mechanical pencil.

Soon after starting work, I took my place on the other side of the recruiting table, particularly the lunch table. I spent many long lunch hours chatting up college students from the local schools and around the world. At the same time, I cheerfully engaged in our unofficial competition to return the largest lunch bill. Instead of three martini lunches, we had three filet mignon lunches, complete with salad and dessert course. Tough job, but I had to do my part to make those recruits want us more than we wanted them.

I had been with the firm a little over a year when I got pregnant. Looking back, I realize the sigh of frustration that must have been sighed behind closed doors. Seventeen years later, I have been on the other side of that pregnancy announcement. I have sighed the sigh, and then felt the guilt that lies behind the sigh, because no one ever knows how a woman will decide to manage her life once there's a baby in it. No one sighed audibly, and if anyone were to have expressed any disappointment at the time, I wouldn't have understood. Of course I was pregnant. I was a married woman in my late-twenties with a fantastic husband, a great job, and a new condo. Why wouldn't I get pregnant? As for what I'd do after the baby came, well naturally I would return to work in my previous capacity. That much was obvious and I wouldn't have expected anyone to expect anything less.

Anyway, I like to imagine the sigh, but that's just ego. After all, at my level I was still extremely interchangeable. That much I knew—which is why I took careful precautions to ensure all would be in good order when I left on maternity leave. I communicated thoroughly and often with my managers. Everybody knew the drill, and despite my husband's joke that I'd leave work on Friday, have the baby, and be back to work Monday morning, I planned to take all my regular maternity leave plus vacation, which would give me about three months off without a gap in pay. With a due date in late August, the little bundle of flannel and I would be roasting a turkey before I had to go back to work.

I like fall, with its new beginnings and new routines. I had studied up on getting a baby to sleep in his own bed, daycare was secured, and I knew how to work the breast pump so my baby would have me even when he didn't have me. I had even practiced. Not on my breasts, but I had all the basic functions down. I created checklists of things we'd need to pack in the car and systems for getting everything done at home and work. I would rock this working mom thing. I had this.

All I had to do was make it official.

On a sunny afternoon in July, I visited the HR department where a nice woman with a blond bob led me into a cubicle and sat with me at a round white table. *We're all equals here*, said the peaceful edge-free surface. She put a manila folder on the table and smiled. This particular agent of our sizable HR department was one who seemed to have neither the company's nor the employees' interests at heart. She operated only as an arbiter of the confusing and convoluted federal regulations. And she had the paperwork that granted thirteen weeks with my newborn. We discussed my plans.

"You know," she said, tucking a stray section of her perfect hair behind her ear, "They don't have to hold your job beyond twelve weeks."

She was talking, of course, about the Family Medical Leave Act, FMLA, the law that states my employers had to give me twelve weeks off—but no more.

Didn't she know my partners loved me? Had word of my brilliance transforming disparate documents into cohesive arguments not made it to her floor? Was she completely ignorant of my prowess with an Access database? I was no ordinary girl with a ten-key.

"They'll hold my job."

"You've discussed this with them?"

"At length."

She appeared confused. "And they are aware you are taking extra time beyond your allotted twelve weeks?"

*Extra time.*

We were discussing a single extra week.

"They are aware," I said.

"Okay, then," she said with just a hint of a shrug. "Sign here."

The next day, I became a new type of recruiter—the maternal type. All the women-are-equal-here yada-yada I'd taken for granted during my own pre-firm days came back to me as I paraded my robust figure in front of a group of college recruits and spouted packaged positivity. I was living, gestating proof of the firm's family-friendliness.

"Lela will be coming back after her maternity and just pick up where she left off," said the HR rep, all smiles and unicorn glaze.

"I'll be back," I said.

But not a minute before the end of that extra week.

They needed me more than I needed them. Right?

# Delivering a Baby in Eight Easy Steps

☙

AFTER MONTHS OF WEIGHT GAIN, hormonal instability, and the alien invasion that is pregnancy, these steps will ensure a painless and joyful delivery, Cesarean-style.

**Step 1: Accept that bed-rest is a scam.**
All those faux contractions and you still made it to 37 weeks. Congratulations! On the bright side, you are now a master at Atari Centipede and proud owner of 65 Pinterest boards about nurseries, Mexican casseroles, and '80s video gaming.

**Step 2: Schedule your induction.**
"Gel induction" sounds like a beauty treatment, but has nothing to do with hair. However, similar to the services of an elite salon, the procedure comes with a complimentary massage. As long as you're not hung up about the particular body part, you'll soon have the most relaxed cervix on the block.

**Step 3: Watch the baby slide right out.**
KIDDING!

**Actual Step 3: Eat Thai food, take a walk, and have sex.**

These tricks might help coax a baby into its final descent, but you have magic gel and a gooey cervix, so simply enjoy your final evening of pregnancy. Before bed, step into that far-cry-from-Pinterest-worthy nursery of yours and smell the pristine baby clothes, because, spoiler alert: Not all babies smell like powder and sunshine. Some of them smell like cheese.

**Step 4: Buy a car.**

Will there ever be a better day to negotiate?

**Step 5: Get an epidural.**

Be still while the stranger inserts a massive needle into your spine. Do not think about paralysis and death. Do not look at your husband as he turns white, starts to sway, and must be removed by an irritated nurse. Once the epidural takes effect, there is no pain and not much for you to do. Your husband, on the other hand, keeps busy in the hall. Car insurance doesn't buy itself.

**Step 6: Surrender.**

Is it you, or is the nurse a little too excited when the doctor finally says "C-Section" aloud? But what harm is a little nervous energy. She has two jobs, this nurse: Count the instruments, and shave you. Worst-case scenario: You leave the hospital with an embedded scalpel and a bad landing strip.

**Step 7: Marvel at the miracle of modern medicine.**
After you have kissed your baby and smelled him and wept at the wonder of life, try not to freak out when you learn that your uterus is outside of your body. Literally laying on your abdomen. That's where they stitch it up. Apparently not all internal organs are securely attached. Who knew?

**Step 8: Weigh yourself.**
Inform the nurses that their scale is in dire need of recalibration because, despite having expelled an eight-and-a-half pound human from your body, you have lost only five pounds.

Then sneak your baby out of the hospital before anyone realizes you have absolutely no idea what you're doing.

# First Stitch

☙

MY MOTHER HAD TOLD ME to rub lanolin on my nipples to "toughen them up" for breastfeeding. This advice was not in any of the many books piled on my nightstand, but Mom promised the sticky wax would help me enjoy the best part of caring for a baby. Nipple massage was the single piece of advice she offered, so I listened, applying the cream religiously, hoping to develop a set of mighty areolas, tough as any plastic facsimile, able to dispense milk at a single squeeze.

Of course, breast prep was just one of the many tasks on my path to motherhood. Other to-dos included coordinating baby outfits, decorating the nursery, and creating a Gant chart for getting my newborn into his crib before the end of my maternity leave. However, contrary to my carefully considered schedules and my macro-enabled spreadsheets, pregnancy did not proceed as planned. A month before my due date, I was put on bed rest. I have since learned that some people don't actually rest in bed while on bed rest, but I was new. An hour after the doctor said lie flat, I was horizontal.

Luckily I remembered I had crafty genes. Throughout the 1970s, my mother made macramé plant hangers and bathing suits. She decoupaged. At one point she was, literally, the seamstress for the band. Mom also crocheted blankets in a Crayola-worthy patchwork of burnt umber, turquoise, and periwinkle. Black, violet, and raspberry crème. She spent hours looping yarn in and out of itself. Suddenly I had hours. Could crochet save me from daytime television and an escalating Tums habit?

I asked my husband to stop by the yarn store after work. He came home with a pearlescent green hook, three skeins of light blue Red Heart Soft Baby yarn, and a slim volume covered with pictures of sweaters and booties.

But crochet was blankets. Those other things were knitting and knitting was hard. It had two needles. My husband pointed out that the booklet was titled *Beginner's Crochet*.

I opened it to find a full page of pencil diagrams. Just like the belly shots in my well-worn volume of *What to Expect When You're Expecting*. In addition to the chain and the V-stitches I recognized, there were dozens of other ways to manipulate yarn: the double, the triple, and the double-triple, naturally. Beyond that, a whole world of puffs, clusters, bobbles, and popcorn stitches. And to interpret this language of yarn: a legend of internationally accepted crochet abbreviations and symbols.

I called my mother immediately. "I thought you knew how to crochet?"

All the blankets my mother had made, the ones she still

had in her bedroom and her living room, and sometimes the kitchen, looked the same: Nubby little fans formed into squares and then patched together to make larger squares. That's it. No puffs, no bobbles, and certainly no popcorn clusters.

"Oh, yes," Mom said. "I used to crochet a lot."

"No, Mom, you didn't crochet. You did one stitch. It's called a granny square. There are like 37 other stitches."

How could she not have told me? Why had she wasted all those years on that one piddly stitch? Why had she not fully examined the fine art of crochet and taught me its intricacies? This was *so* like my mother. Just like she didn't teach me that rice doesn't always come with a-Roni? Or that you're only supposed to "enhance" a beauty mark if you already *have* a beauty mark? Or that kitchen sponges are, in fact, disposable? And even now, after having two babies of her own, the sum total of her advice was to rub myself with lanolin.

"Mom, there are instructions and patterns! You can make stuff. Sweaters even. With sleeves! And by the way, it's called an afghan. Why didn't you tell me?"

She was quiet for a moment before she answered. "I didn't know."

She didn't know.

Just like she didn't know at seventeen, far from home and laboring among strangers, what kind of daughter I would become: ambitious, fiercely independent, a bit of a know-it-all, and before all that, colicky.

Most of the stitches in my newfound universe of crochet were simply variations on what I now knew to be the basic half-double. I picked them up quickly, having watched my mother's wrists dance with the hook and yarn all those years, and spent weeks making blankets and tiny sweaters and booties that almost matched.

All the while I tortured myself with lanolin, which did not actually toughen my nipples as much as it prepared me to endure the agonizing horror that would be the first two weeks of breastfeeding. But I am grateful I listened, because my mother was right.

In time, breastfeeding got easier, and then it got wonderful. Eventually my son and I would learn to nurse blissfully day and night, under the softest blue blanket made from an abundance of stitches my mother gave me. Even though she never knew they existed.

# The Evolution of Breastfeeding, aka Babies Suck

☙

I PAINTED A SWEET PICTURE of nursing, but before all that easy suckling comes the very, very hard part. Before that comes the part where you are a clueless blank slate who believes whomever gets their literature to you first. Here's where, in my case, the La Leche League stepped in to help. Not literally. I didn't go to any meetings or actually read any of their pamphlets, but their dogma had seeped into my consciousness. Failing to breastfeed my baby for twelve to thirty-six months was as good as smothering him with a pillow—that's the power of La Leche's cultural influence. And rightly so. Breastfeeding is a good thing. Encouraging women to breastfeed is a good thing. Indeed breast is best. However, sometimes good enough is best, and other times your best just isn't good enough. And that's okay, too. But you don't tell that to the La Leche Mafia, and you don't tell it to the woman who amassed a parenting library before the pregnancy test was out of the wrapper.

There would be no nipple facsimile for my Zander.

Everyone knew that a newborn subjected to a hospital-issue pacifier would surely reject his mother's breast in favor of the lifeless nub of silicone. I made sure the nurses knew I wasn't going to make that rookie mistake. (Section 3.6, paragraph ii of the Birth Plan.) They humored me for a full twelve hours. That's how long my resolve lasted because, incidentally, that's how long my son cried after his entrance into the world. That grating sound got old fast—for me *and* for the nurses, who asked, begged, and bribed me to give the kid a binky.

"Fine, give him the pacifier," I said, finally giving in and grieving my first maternal defeat.

I got over it.

Turns out La Leche deals in half-truths. My son wanted the pacifier, sure. Who wouldn't? But he also wanted the breast. The militant stance against pacifiers or bottles was crap, and fearmongering about how a breast pump damages your ability to produce enough milk was a lie. Here's the truth: Your baby wants your breasts. Contrary to our societal obsession with cleavage, that's why they exist. The rest is details.

Unfortunately, the only training for breastfeeding is on-the-job training. You can read about it, you can practice with a willing spouse, you can go to town with lanolin, but nothing can really prepare you for the challenge of providing actual sustenance to a helpless human being. Spoiler alert: He doesn't know what he's doing, either. After accepting defeat on the pacifier front, I attempted to redeem myself by attending the hospital's lactation class where I learned and practiced the football hold and the cradle hold. Then I took the class again. Same class, same instruction. If they'd had a remedial course I would have taken that, too, because I needed all the help I could get. And it worked. Slowly, awkwardly, my son and I got comfortable enough that he actually took in some nourishment.

This gig could only get easier, right?

As the Mommy, there are certain things no one else can do for you. No one can toughen up your nipples. No one can get that milk to come down when there is not enough, or express it when there is too much. No one can change your milk-soaked shirt. Being the mommy is really, really hard, even when you have a partner who adores you and your baby. There is a fine line between scaring new moms and telling the whole truth, but if we're ready to have a baby, we are ready to hear how profoundly that baby will change our lives, and not always for the better.

The truth is that babies suck.

One evening while I was settling onto the couch for the 48th feeding of the day (did you know breastfed babies feed every 17 minutes?), my husband, John, tried to help me get comfortable.

"Could you get me a glass of water?" I asked. And while I'd like to say I said please, let's be real. He got me a glass of water.

"Can you pass me the notebook?"

Documentation was critical to the process. He passed the notebook.

"Can you bring my pillow? The hard one, not the squishy one."

He brought the pillow.

"Can you turn on the light? And turn down the TV? And get that damn cat away from me!"

He complied on all counts.

Once Zander locked his death grip on my battered nipple and started the cheese-grating action that was our early nursing pattern, the pain got the better of me.

"Oh my god, can't you help me at all? I'm doing *everything*!"

At the time, the statement seemed true. In that moment where you are the only one who can provide your baby what he wants, what he needs, you are doing everything. While I was pregnant, I never imagined myself as a newbie mother, but more of an apprentice studying to master the art of motherhood with a fierce determination to do everything right. I would be a ninja of all things newborn.

When my maternity leave ended, a new daily routine began. I returned to analyzing transactions and running database queries. I was also in charge of daycare drop-off, nursing at lunch, and expressing liquid gold from my breasts at regular intervals during the workday. Before leaving the condo every morning, I consulted a packing list that included any work I'd been finishing the night before, diapers, wipes, changes of clothing (for Zander), the sweater I put on for the lunch hour nursing dates (I was like a lactating Fred Rogers), Vaseline, empty bottles, formula, pacifiers, back-up pacifiers, frozen gel packs, and the breast pump. I carried four bags: a laptop case, a purse, a diaper bag, and the insulated carrying system for the breast pump.

I worked hard to maintain my milk supply, pumping twice a day. As part of the firm's keep-women-on-board campaign, I had access to a dedicated lounge complete with a self-serve espresso machine and private rooms for discreet milking. Although I indulged in nursing-break lattes, the milk going in did not equate to milk coming out, but I kept at it, later transferring my hard-earned ounce or two into plastic bags to freeze, or mixing it with formula straight into a bottle for Zander to have the next day. When I finished pumping, I'd head back up to my floor, passing through the rich landing lined in dark wood and decorated with tasteful furniture, a Persian carpet, and the best fake Boston fern in Seattle. There was a portico around the big mahogany doors, and above that, in classic, understated script, in big brass letters: Arthur Andersen. Seeing that gave me a fresh a shot of external validation every time. This was where I belonged. I knew it the first time I'd come to interview. All the studying, the competition, the endless recruiting events, the grunt duties of a first year staff had all paid off. Here I was three years later, just another trusted colleague on a lactation break.

One day, a young guy got into the elevator with me. He nodded and looked at my bag with competitive curiosity in his eyes. I had something he wanted.

"Is that the new laptop?"

There were two ways to play this. Let him believe that I was one of the privileged few with the new computer, and the new bag, or tell the truth.

I chose shock value.

"This?" I held up my bag.

# Living the Dream?

❦

THERE WAS NEVER ANY QUESTION Zander would be in daycare. During my first trimester, we shopped for one. First I looked downtown, near my office. Ideally, I wanted something within walking distance to make it easier to nurse Zander at lunchtime. I pictured myself dropping him off in the morning and retrieving him in the afternoon, all while impeccably dressed and carrying a smart-looking laptop bag. John and I spent many lunch hours walking around in the rain from daycare to daycare, looking for a place that offered infant care through Kindergarten. By the thirteenth week of my pregnancy, we'd narrowed our search down to two, either of which would cost half my salary.

The first childcare provider was just a few blocks from my office. The downtown location was ideal, despite being in a decrepit and damp building that shook with Seattle's frequent small earthquakes. The place smelled of crayons, and its bright cubbies reminded me of my own preschool days. The director was a soft, sweet woman in a patchwork skirt. The second place was a mile away, housed in a Japanese nursing home, or "intergenerational facility." Kids in one wing; seniors in another. The building was new and secure, and sat peacefully on a hill above the hustle of downtown. Just inside, a rice paper door slid open to reveal a miniature tearoom where the children learned to be still and to observe the power of rituals, mostly snack and story times. (And presumably not to do any weird geisha stuff.) No shoes allowed. This was the closer. We got our as-yet-unborn baby on the list just in time for a spot after my maternity leave ended.

Cut to nine months later: I was headed back to the job my partners had so graciously held for me. The daycare drill began. Each morning, I drove the new Ford Explorer down 2nd Avenue and up Yesler, praying for green lights all the way because Zander cried at every single red. Once there, I hauled him and all his gear into the cozy little room where he spent the day making a mess for someone else to clean up. Usually, that someone was Maria, the primary caregiver in the infant room, a young Hispanic mother who nonchalantly handled multiple simultaneous diaper changes, feedings, naps, and tummy times. The woman was born maternal.

Getting Zander settled at daycare was the easy part. They had a system, part State of Washington childcare regulations and part ancient Japanese secret. John picked him up in the afternoon while I made up the work time I'd lost to extracting fluids from my body and putting them into a holding tank or a real boy. Dinners consisted of Hamburger Helper and frozen lasagna, which didn't exactly help the pounds melt off. After that, we executed the bedtime routine and caught up on the day's work.

This was living the dream.

Most days I visited the daycare at lunchtime, changing into a sweater I kept in the car to protect myself from Zander's adorable spit up, and tried to nurse. But many days, I missed the opportunity by five minutes because Maria thought Zander was "just too hungry to wait for Mommy." Choosing my battles took on new meaning as I resisted telling Maria exactly what I thought of her feeding policies. Then again, maybe Zander really couldn't wait. I had to trust that she knew best what he needed in the moment I was busy tweaking a formula or lining up pie charts in PowerPoint. I had to trust that Maria knew when my son was too hungry to wait and when he could have waited for five more minutes, because *are you kidding me*?

Regardless, I spent many a lunch hour coaxing Zander into breastfeeding when he may or may not have been full from the bottle. Whether he filled up on the bottle or the breast, Zander saved his spit-up for me. Despite my clever sweater, I returned to the office every day smelling like aged feta, but also satisfied that I wasn't really missing out on any of his formative milestones. After all, Maria kept me apprised of all the important things in a daily log, which included everything that went into my baby and how it came out.

One day when I showed up at daycare at noon, covered in a week's worth of my own milk and distracted by an overdue report, Maria cheerfully told me about Zander's morning. Among the news of his smiles and kicking and smearing of rice cereal was this gem:

"He loves lemonade!"

*Excuse me?*

My son was six months old. This was Seattle, where even if you didn't know a BPA from an IPA, you at least aspired to provide the illusion of holistic health. Zander had consumed five things in his entire life: breast milk, formula, rice cereal, peas, and sweet potatoes. The last two were homemade, not because I was entirely controlling or entirely organic, but because I was entirely practical and practically poor. Even though John and I were fully employed, college educated professionals, we were making barely enough to cover the mortgage and necessities. We lived in the cheapest house in a great neighborhood, and it still took an entire paycheck to cover the mortgage. And almost half of my income was now going to childcare, where my baby's new mommy was apparently having all the fun.

*Lemonade, anyone?*

"Oh, yes, he loves it!" Maria said in response to my stunned silence.

She explained how she had brought her drive-thru breakfast into work, and—so much for sanitary procedures—how she dipped her finger into her drink and gave it to Zander.

That should have been me.

Didn't she know I was saving stuff like that?

Who the hell did she think she was, bonding with my baby?

Giving Zander something new to try belonged to John and me. Maria had stolen a moment we could never recover. Most important, why should she get credit in his impressionable psyche for being the bearer of his first blessed taste of refined white sugar?

But this was what we chose. There was no way to go but forward. The regular daily routine was ripe for disruption. Before Zander was born I signed up for a class at the firm's training facility outside of Chicago. I prepared for months, packing the freezer with breast milk and making checklists for everything from getting Zander dressed to packing his diaper bag to his bath schedule. John's parents were coming to help. The first few days went well, relaxing even. I attended classes, ate cafeteria food, and slept in the narrower-than-single size bed in my dorm-style room at St. Charles. I had free time to work out in the gym. It was bliss.

The last night at St. Charles, there was live music at the bar onsite. Just-out-of-college aged kids from all over the world drank and danced. I swayed along, trying to calculate how long I had until signs of lactation pegged me as the odd woman on the dance floor. The musical act was a local guy who sold cassette tapes after the show from a small table in front of the stage. I bought one.

"So what's your story?" he asked.

"My story?"

"What do you do?"

I launched into the description of the services provided by the Economic and Financial Consulting Group. He looked confused and told me I was the first person he'd ever met in all his years performing at St. Charles who actually wanted to be an accountant. Everybody else was just marking time, making money to finance their real dreams. Apparently, I was surrounded by artists, musicians, and poets. My love of spreadsheets suddenly felt misguided. I finished my beer, went back to my tiny room, and pumped breast milk into the sink.

A week after I got home, before I had fully unpacked from the Chicago trip, I was assigned to a project in Phoenix. It was a quickie and I was excited to have the opportunity, but hated to travel. And this time, instead of having months to plan, re-plan, and over-plan both my own time away and my family's time at home without me, I had only a few days to get things in order. John's parents came to Seattle again and off I went to Phoenix, where my travel companion kindly indulged our mutual binge listening of the cassette I'd bought in Chicago. Over and over the lyrics challenged me. Every song seemed to be about doing something else, somewhere else. I started to feel crushed under the overwhelming feeling that I was doing this mommy thing all wrong.

One night, midweek, as I sat at the little hotel table with a pile of documents and a Styrofoam container of Thai food to sustain me through the hours of work ahead, I called home. John and I talked about our days, but the only thing on my mind was how I could continue to work such an uncertain schedule. I didn't want to be that girl who took herself out of the rotation for every good project. How could I advance if I did that? I knew, too, that it wasn't just the erratic travel that would wear me down, but also the long hours, and the struggle to stay connected while missing every collegial lunch to feed my son. Add to this my inexperience negotiating domestic affairs with a man whose mother still folded his underwear when she came to visit. The work of keeping our family alive and clean was never-ending, and I was never doing any of it right. I'd already had a near miss with a total breakdown when I dropped a hot casserole on the kitchen floor. That night, when I heard Zander in the background, I decided the time had come to leave my job.

In one of my initial interviews with the firm, a partner had told me, "We don't put pressure on anyone here. We hire the type of people who put pressure on themselves."

I had put pressure on myself, and I had come up short.

In retrospect, it's easy to think I could have made it work if I had wanted to. What I was unable to admit then, what is even hard to admit now, is that I didn't want it badly enough. But I didn't want to be a stay-at-home mom, either. And if you'd asked me then, I could not have said I was putting my family first, even though that's exactly what I was doing. I simply could not handle the stress of being pulled in two directions, even when I was the one doing the pulling.

I wanted to be the Woman Who Had It All. I just wasn't willing to be the Woman Who Cried on the Kitchen Floor in order to get it.

I needed an exit strategy.

# Stay Home, Mom

❦

WHEN I DECIDED TO LEAVE, the partners kept the door open for me to work on projects on an hourly basis. As a senior analyst, I had skills they didn't want to lose. They had invested in me, and my leaving presented an opportunity for the firm to employ me on a contract basis as needed. Win-win.

"Maybe when your son goes to Kindergarten you'll come back," one partner had said.

Kindergarten seemed like forever in the future. Part of me just wanted a clean break, but another part knew money was going to be insanely tight. Yet another part of me suspected this Mommy gig was going to spell my death. Still, I didn't want to close any doors. I wrote a memo detailing my ideal world—working for the firm from home, 10-15 hours a week, with no travel. The partners were honest that projects that fit my criteria could be scarce, but we kept the door open.

I told all of this to the HR rep, the same one who had cautioned me about my excessive beyond-FMLA week of maternity leave.

"The partners don't really like that kind of thing," she said.

Which seemed weird, considering it was their idea.

She processed my paperwork while I stared at the carpeted walls of the cubicle.

A week later, our division gathered for drinks at a bar around the corner from the office for my official going away party. We shared a lot of beverages, a lot of laughs, and a lot stories about awful projects and travel mishaps. My favorite: the time another staffer and I had missed our flight home from San Francisco—while sitting at the gate. The only partner who showed up was my current favorite: the one who had called me a hard-ass when I criticized a new recruit; put my attitude in check in a formative moment when he told me that, in the short term, he expected me to do "anything short of shoveling shit" to get the job done; and pushed through my promotion. Perhaps most endearing, though, was his praise about the first project I handled all by myself, a rebuttal of imaginary lost profits in a litigation over a certain South American lottery gone wrong: "You've made a silk purse out of a sow's ear."

"We're really going to miss you," he said now.

I reminded him of the plan we had made. "You can't get rid of me so easily."

"That's odd," he said. "Because I requested you for a project last week. HR said it wouldn't work out."

Of course they did.

But a going-away party wasn't the time to think about such things, and the next day I didn't care. I wanted clarity, not fuzzy lines of complicated working arrangements and difficult HR negotiations. I needed to sell myself on the idea of being a stay-at-home mom. So I let it go. I went home and tried to enjoy my baby.

Our house was small, but with the baby, and my new title of Stay Home Mom, it felt like a lot—enough to put into a spreadsheet, anyway. Filling in rectangles with the tasks that would occupy long days helped me feel in control. An overachiever needs to achieve, after all. No one can argue that nurturing a human being is not a worthy accomplishment, but the work is never done. Tasks on the to-do list are never completely checked off.

On the upside, I still had the "new moms" group I'd bonded with during Zander's first ten weeks. They welcomed me back with open arms and we resumed our ritual of laying the babies on the floor in a circle, and taking turns talking about our week. I had my petty concerns: diaper rash, losing too many binkies, only wanting sex with the light off. I did not mention if I had not left the house that week, or if I'd spent two whole days in a row plastered to the couch, getting up only when Zander needed something. I tried not to lament that my entire life had become one long baby schedule. I was one of the lucky ones now. I got to stay home with my baby. And come on, it wasn't that hard. Certainly easier than getting all this stuff done and also having a job.

That's what I told myself.

I soon found that watching more than one episode of Martha Stewart in a day is cause for concern, but watching more than three means someone should put you on suicide watch. I knew it was time for a change when I started foraging in the backyard for the makings of jam. Approximately two months in, I hit the wall. I simply could not take another day of staring at that same baby face and seeking fulfillment in home and hearth. When John suggested I get a part-time job as a bookkeeper, I assured him in a tone of utter disgust that, "I did not become a CPA so I could be a bookkeeper."

In fact, I was a terrible bookkeeper and only passed the required electronic bookkeeping class in college because the professor gave me a second chance to complete the class's single, semester-long assignment, which I had failed because I hated making things balance. I wanted other people to do that. I wanted to boss those people around and write reports and meet with clients. So I found Zander a lovely new daycare and went back to the firm, to the place where most CPA mommies go: the tax department.

There I helped employees of and investors in Microsoft decide when to exercise their stock options. From the comfort of a window cubicle, I built detailed financial models to pinpoint the precise moment the soon-to-be financially elite should retire. In this new role, I reported to a bright young MBA who was and remains the only person I have ever known to use the word *machinations* in a sentence. There were machinations in my spreadsheets, machinations in the supporting documents for the tax returns I helped to prepare, and most important, machinations in the free markets that would determine the fortunes of the young millionaires we served.

My only purpose in client meetings was to sit quietly

and increase the firm's presence in the room. That's how we justified our rates. I jotted down the occasional note, whether or not one was needed, to give the dual impressions that what the client said was extremely important, and that the brains of my boss, and her boss, and everybody's boss, aka our partner, were engaged in such deep and important thoughts that they certainly couldn't be interrupted with taking a note. We worked hard to imply that these thoughts were definitely happening at a level far above the abilities of the client's meager mental acuity. A week later, we would present him with his six-inch-thick return and a PowerPoint complete with multiple target date retirement scenarios. After he left, grinning at his incredible fortune, a partner would tap the tax return and say, "This is what we do. We make their financial lives so complex that they never leave."

Like a script.

I remembered something I'd been told during my internship at another firm. A young woman said she had to do some kind of charity work to offset the feeling that her only purpose in life was to make rich people richer. I felt that, and worse, that I'd become just another mommy-tracked assistant. I was already questioning the wisdom of coming back to the firm, and especially of switching departments, when I got pregnant again. My due date was a month after April 15th. If I stayed I'd be gigantic and uncomfortable all of tax season.

Still, the money. We needed it.

I had an idea. A wonderful awful idea.

I resigned from the firm (again) and printed out a

poorly designed flyer and a cheap business card. LD Financial was born. I might have been successful if I had spent more time hustling clients and less time designing the amateurish brochure. I had a box printed and sent a hundred brochures to addresses in the neighborhood. That's how I got my client. Just the one.

And let's agree not to call it bookkeeping, shall we?

My husband's career was in flux and that one client of mine wasn't exactly bridging the financial gap. We were desperate to get out of our crippling mortgage, and at the same time, needed more space. There was no way we could afford to stay in the city. If we moved to the suburbs, the east side of Seattle, we'd have to find all new friends. And moving was moving after all. John started looking for a new job, opening up his search to other parts of the country. A week later, we got the call from Wichita Falls, Texas, a town distinguished by once having been home to the highest number of millionaires per capita, and holding the world records for teenage pregnancy and the number of days over 108 degrees.

That's when my career in stay-home motherhood really began.

Sort of.

# Apology to a Second Child

⚬

DEAREST DAUGHTER,

This letter is long overdue. I have needed to send it since you were about 8 and started asking the very appropriate question, "When can we watch the home movies with me in them?"

About that...

You see, when your brother was a baby, we had nothing better to do than watch his every move, notice the subtleties of his growth and development, and marvel at the wonder that we had created another human being. That is seriously fascinating—the first time.

Compounding our obsession with capturing your brother's every coo and gurgle was the technological feat known as the Sony Handycam. At 13 pounds and the size of a Mini-Cooper, this personal movie camera was standard issue for over-archiving urban parents. And yes, we plead guilty to excessive documentation of your brother's first years.

Contrast that with your early years. When you were a baby, we were busy being a family. There was a lot less time to take all those home movies. We didn't have a camera in every phone. We had to plug the damn thing in. We had to buy cartridges. And frankly, even if we'd had cameras in our pockets, let's be honest: We had been down Baby Lane. Don't take this the wrong way—you have many fine qualities your brother will never possess—but by the time you were born, we realized that babies just aren't that interesting. Your adorable noises, your crazy baby faces, your early attempts at "mama" and "baba" weren't something we felt compelled to preserve for future generations.

It wasn't you; it was us.

So, yes, your baby book is not quite as full as your brother's, and your feature films are sparse. But there is one piece of your history that we didn't skimp on. In fact, your brother doesn't even have one of these, because he didn't have a doula. And yours made you a very special photo album. After taking you home from the hospital, as we were settling in and making our way through the freezer full of casseroles, my doula—your doula—dropped by with a small photo album filled with all manner of thoughtfully captured visual mementos of my hours in labor.

Now, you may be wondering why you have never seen this very special album. That is because it is, shall we say, explicit. Doulas are shameless like that. They will take a picture of anything. Especially the thing with the baby coming out of it. But don't worry, Sweetheart. You got cut out of me with a big knife and they didn't allow cameras in the operating room.

The album is actually a really nice travelogue, if you will, of the day you journeyed into the land of fully formed humans. For example, there's a great shot of me in the car with my trusty blue bowl, because nausea is a hazard of labor. And yes, if you're wondering, it is supremely humbling to vomit in front anyone who is not your mother. (You may or may not experience this firsthand during your college years.) I'm counting your father as a friend here, even though he wasn't too friendly toward me over the whole VBAC debacle. (Spoiler alert: It didn't work!) You know what's worse than puking among friends? Lying naked in a hospital tub while moaning like a cow as your friends stand by and watch. That attractive look is also documented in your special book.

Feeling pretty superior to your brother now, aren't you?

You see, I had a grand idea to labor in water, because I had a doula and because I lived in Seattle. So, very soon after arriving at the hospital—I'm sorry, *birthing center*—I lowered my girth into a tub of warm water and proceeded to engage in deep breathing. Your father was very helpful. He is a great breather. There are some photos in the album of him looking very patient.

I stayed in the water as long as I could before it got too cold, and then I moved to the bed, where your doula captured some lovely shots of me in all sorts of positions—all failed attempts to "get comfortable." Those where I have that very pained look on my face are probably the times the nurse was trying to get you to turn around in my womb. Oh, you didn't know that either? Yes, dear, just like your brother before you, you thought it would be cute to play hide-and-seek. Except we could all see you, and it really hurt, and I wished you would just turn around already and slide on out.

That was not going to happen.

Instead I spent many hours laboring before you finally came out by Cesarean section, or what I like to call "the easy way." (Don't get mad at me, crunchy Earth ladies and Jessica Alba. My hips were not made for baby-making and I married a man with a very large head.)

In the background of such dainty compositions as "Woman with Leg Askew" and "Man Trying to Comfort Moaning Wife," you may notice the décor of the hospital room. I have no idea why they try to make those rooms look like "home," but I don't like it. Not that you asked. I wouldn't want to have my appendix removed in a room that looked like a den, and it wasn't great for having a baby, either. Once I got in the car with a bowl, I wanted a medical environment, filled with people who could ease my pain and extract my baby. Not a needlepoint pillow and a cross-stitched platitude. If the look is supposed to be relaxing, they're underestimating the discomfort that is labor. Do they think we'll be so soothed we will forget why we're there?

*Oh, look, a love seat! Let's kick back and watch* American Idol.

In summary, I am sorry that there aren't many pictures, and likely no movies, of you trying to find your mouth with a banana. But there is a beautiful image of you in the OR, just after the nurses massaged and prodded you into the world of the living. You are crying, which is a great sign in a newborn. Dad is stroking your head, which is huge. Picture a really big, soft, baby bobblehead doll.

And then there you are at my breast.

I'm crying. Because it hurts. But also because I am so excited that I have a baby girl. I hadn't dared to wish for such luck.

After that, all the pictures are of you and your brother. You two have been inseparable ever since.

He must have pushed you out of frame when the camcorder started rolling.

Forgive us all,
Mother

# Culture Shock

❦

MOVING FROM WASHINGTON to the Bible Belt was a Texas-sized adjustment. Along with new manners, climate, and standards of dress, I had to learn a whole new genre of joke: the Baptist joke. As in, *Why do you always have to take two Baptists fishing? Because if you just take one, he'll drink all your beer.* No matter your stance on whether Texas is part of the South, the West, or just Texas, when you are from the West Coast, Texas is very Southern. So is Oklahoma, but I'm not going to pick that fight. Luckily I had a big new house to offset the culture shock.

The first time I saw my home in Texas was the day I arrived with a toddler and a baby, long after the papers had been signed. John and I had been unable to find something suitable on our one and only house-hunting trip, despite the talents of our realtor. Tami-with-an-*i* was a 38-year-old grandmother with a slow, thick drawl and a penchant for unpainted wood cabinetry ("Y'all… that's red oak!"). With the exotic lumber spoken for, I went back to Seattle to pack while Tami and John found our perfect house. So what if two years earlier the area had been nothing but a canyon filled with rattlers and scorpions? At nearly 2,500 square feet, this house was more than double the size of our dry-rotted mess of a cottage in Seattle, *and* it had two bathrooms. The luxury! More income and a smaller mortgage would translate to less stress over all the things we didn't have. It felt exciting, but I harbored another feeling, too: dread. I couldn't envision my days ahead. In Texas I knew no one. No one knew me. Although I knew it was irrational, I couldn't shake the feeling that I would literally cease to exist, fade into the nothingness of Middle America.

However, I had a plan. I would join the Junior League, which I knew nothing about, other than that they held fundraisers and worked for charitable causes. I decided this association would help me become established, make friends, and ensure a built-in network for the next time we moved, which we expected to become a regular thing.

Once the kids and I made it to Texas, I was too busy changing diapers and unpacking to worry about making friends and doing good. The kids and I tried to get out and do things, but had hard time structuring our days around the heat and the tarantula sightings. If we wanted to go to the park, we had to get there by 7:30 in the morning—before the temperature rose to the typical 108 degree high. Sometimes we hit the air conditioning at the library. On those days, I'd go to the only drive-through coffee place in town. It was called The Coffee Man, which was also how the gentleman who owned the place referred to himself. He was also the only black person my children ever saw, not because there were few black people in Wichita Falls, but because the town is '60s-era segregated. This wasn't so different from my childhood in the Pacific Northwest, where the only African-Americans I knew were the Jeffersons, the Cosbys, and the family from *Good Times*. Once I got out of my small town, I forgot all about never knowing people of different races. But in Texas, we moved back into a bubble of good jobs, granite countertops, and aspirations to be in the Junior League.

And white people.

That's where we lived. I had no idea where the coffee man lived, but this was the South, after all, and I was too busy to concern myself with time warps and casual racism. I had kids to raise.

I might never have made it to the Junior League if I had not been sitting on the couch at just the right time one fateful day. I spotted a woman walking by the house. A quick assessment through strategically tilted plantation blinds revealed she was about my age and had a boy and a girl about my kids' ages, too. Jackpot! I ran to the bedroom, changed into a clean t-shirt, and raced out to pounce on this critical social interaction. Our long walkway made my faux-nonchalance extra awkward. It's hard to look casual when you're sprinting toward a stranger.

"Oh, hi!" I tried not to knock her down with my lonely enthusiasm. "I was just um… checking the mail."

What were the odds that this fortuitous stranger would be a member in good standing of the Junior League? Apparently I have excellent stalking skills. Allyson invited me to an informational membership meeting. When I said, "Yes, oh HELL yes," Allyson sponsored me and recruited three of her friends to do the same so that I could be offered membership into this elite group, the organization of choice for local doctors' wives, professional women, and others who employed decorators and shopped in boutiques. Considering I'd nearly run Allyson down while she was trying to take a walk with her kids, this seemed like rather a generous gesture. In the South, this is known as hospitality.

My days took on a new lightness now that I had guaranteed, scheduled girl time on the calendar. And I learned things from my new friends, like who the good pediatricians were and how to *not* do your grocery shopping in the midday heat because sooner or later you had to leave the hypercooled aisles and load up the car.

My friends today occasionally remind to use my "Southern girl filter," which after all these years away from the Coast, still eludes me. But I swear I did try to learn the ways of the Southern girls. I may not have bothered with labeling food at a party, and I never learned to wear jewelry at the pool, but I made my own slow progress toward Southernization. In time, I learned to have dish towels monogrammed and to search for home accents (never enough home décor) at Hobby Lobby, where I was, naturally, guaranteed not to see anyone who was not white.

On a morning Walmart run, the bubble we lived in became embarrassingly clear. I had my 2- and 4-year-olds in one of those monster double stroller/carts I had grown to love. As I pushed the cart past a mostly empty row, Zander pointed to a single man browsing the shelves—a black man.

"Mommy, look!" he said. "The Coffee Man!"

But the man was not *our* Coffee Man.

He smiled and shook his head only slightly while I smiled and shrunk to the size of a coffee bean. How could I convey to this man that I did not teach my children to equate the color of one's skin to food and beverage? Should I have explained that the only other black person my son had ever met was in fact called The Coffee Man? Instead I rolled away, just hoping to get my shopping done before the sun rose too high in the sky.

At the end of the year, the Junior League held an annual dinner in the ballroom of the Wichita Falls Country Club, where I reflected upon the fruits of my as-yet-incomplete Southern education. I had collected canned food, sung in a nursing home, sold cookbooks, learned to run a committee, match the nametags to the invitations, and serve something salty, something sweet, and a soda. Sitting at a beautifully set table with my new best friends, I realized I had also adopted the local dress in my lovely periwinkle linen blouse and matching Capri pants, adorned ever so subtly with ribbons, beads, and lace. And I wasn't sure how I felt about that.

For better and worse, I had a lot more to learn about the South.

# How to Take Perfect Family Portraits
# in Nine Easy Steps

❦

EVERY FAMILY NEEDS A PORTRAIT. Not some scrappy snap-shot or iPhone outtake. I'm talking about a professionally lit, awkwardly staged, otherworldly retouched masterpiece mounted on canvas and prominently displayed kind of photo. Also ideal for Christmas cards, graduation announcements, and office walls and desks. Capturing the perfect shot is not easy. There are angles to manipulate and expressions to coax. Perhaps more important are the attitudes to fake. Follow these easy steps for a perfect family portrait.

**Step 1: Plan an expensive vacation to an exotic locale.**

Spare no expense on your destination. Nothing makes your family more attractive than an ocean in the background. Whoever sees the photo will know that you spent a small fortune getting your family to the shores of Costa Rica or the beaches of Barbados. That's impressive. But beaches are not the only acceptable backdrops for a great family portrait.

Architectural structures, such as grand doorways or hearths, speak equally to your family's prosperity and good fortune. If you cannot afford to travel for your family photo and you live in a less than stately home, sneak into the backyard of some more successful neighbor, preferably one who employs a professional landscaping service.

**Step 2: Shop for matching clothing.**

For a beach shot, you will want to wear white linen tops and breezy khakis. Never mind the quality. You will only be wearing these clothes once. They will be destroyed while trying to get the ideal casual shot, which actually takes ninety minutes, four light reflectors, and two different photographers, to say nothing of the small army of support staff required for truly candid looks.

**Step 3: Hire a photographer.**

It is important to encapsulate the essence of the family in the portrait. Only a truly skilled photographer will be equally adept at handling toddler meltdown and teen angst. Coaxing a smile from a surly 13-year-old takes more than a cooing voice and a clever teddy. And only the most gifted professional can quell the long-standing marital issues that surface in times of extreme stress—like when you are having your picture taken next to a toddler who wants juice.

**Step 4: Get ready for your close-up.**

Grooming is critical to your carefully crafted "casual" look. Men and children are easy to manage, requiring only cleanliness and perhaps a last-minute touch up with the original gel, mama's spit. As for your own makeup, keep it simple. This is not the time to try the new eye shadow technique you saw at on a 22-year-old model at Sephora. Do not wear your brand new lipgloss in Raging Orchid. As for hair, console yourself with the fact that hair always looks better in pictures than in the mirror.

**Step 5: Commence the photo shoot.**

Everyone knows a family vacation is not as much a vacation as it is an unwinnable battle to entertain children, negotiate meal plans, and avoid committing homicide while trapped in confined quarters with immediate family. Therefore, it is best not to allow too much time to lapse between arriving at your photographic location and taking the family portrait. Also, you will surely be thinner at the beginning of the vacation than at the end.

**Step 6: Manage unexpected setbacks.**

To get a good family portrait, you must be single-minded. Do not allow minor emergencies to derail your determination. If, for example, one of your family members has a sudden case of food-borne illness, this is not a reason to delay taking the portrait. Remember, anything can be fixed in Photoshop. In a pinch, grab another kid off the beach who is approximately the same height. Chances are he will be happier taking a picture with you than with his own family, and your friends will never know the difference.

**Step 7: Review the proofs.**

Be grateful for all the terrible shots. In some you will look mad. In some you will look goofy. In some you will look like your mother. While these confrontations with unattractive images are damaging to the ego, they also keep you out of bankruptcy court.

**Step 8: Frame and hang.**

Couples often underestimate the strength of feelings about whether or not family portraits belong over the fireplace, and the topic is not often covered in premarital counseling. Consider hiring a professional arbitration specialist to help you navigate the potentially marriage-ending negotiations.

**Step 9: Send the holiday cards.**

Finally, print and send the holiday cards, because what's the point of going through all this trouble if you can't show the world how happy, successful, and attractive you are? All the effort will pay off knowing a cheap copy of your family portrait, framed in crosses, candy canes, and dreidels, is stuck to the refrigerator of some barely remembered acquaintance across the country—next to a lesser family's picture. Enjoy the satisfaction, and then start planning next year's portrait.

# Got Passion?

❦

IN AN OPRAH-INSPIRED QUEST, I decided to revisit the only thing close to a passion I could remember: theater. Drama had sustained me through high school, and I'd considered applying to a university theater program, but the paperwork just piled up in my bedroom, too overwhelming and intimidating to tackle. Over the years, I saw how those theater majors lived: cobbling together a living by busting their asses at odd jobs for the privilege of performing to less-than-full houses in Portland. I chose the path with the regular paycheck and the supplementary life insurance. Maybe I'd made the wrong choice. Maybe acting was my true passion. I owed it to myself to find out.

I auditioned for the next production of the local community theater. A quick Internet search refreshed all my dormant acting knowledge. I would get the part by staying in character for the entire audition, reacting as the other actors read their parts.

Nailed it! The play was Edward Albee's "Three Tall Women." There are only three roles in the play, and they are all the same woman, but at three different ages. So I was playing, for my post-high school theatrical debut, a tall woman at the Backdoor Theater in Wichita Falls, Texas. The luck.

"You were the only one up there who could act," the director told me at our first rehearsal.

Linda had been a regular in the thriving Wichita Falls theater scene before heading west to make her mark on Hollywood. She may not have become a household name, but had a good time trying. Now, back in town to care for her ailing mother, she decided to maintain her sanity by making her directorial debut. She would play the middle-aged tall woman. Sylvia, who played the oldest tall woman, was a lovely veteran of the local theater. Linda was desperate to impress her old thespian friends, I wanted to find my passion, and Sylvia had a bad knee. Not exactly a Tony moment in the making.

During the rehearsals, I was cast in a commercial for a local bank. This passion was seriously starting to pay off. I spent an afternoon dressed in my best business casual, walking back and forth in front of a roll of white butcher paper, swinging a shopping bag. There are worse ways to make fifty dollars.

Unlike high school productions, which culminated in a maximum of two performances—one during school hours and one evening show—this play had a three-week run. After a month and a half of rehearsals, we were scheduled to perform Thursday, Friday, and Saturday nights and Sunday afternoons for nearly a month. The bright side: Nerves meant

I ate a lot less for dinner before I left for the theater on performance nights, so I shed the final pregnancy pounds. The dark side: I had to say the same things twelve times over. I detest repeating myself. Ask my husband.

At the final performance, a young woman approached me with compliments and anxiety. I recognized her from the auditions, and later that night learned she had played the lead in most of the Backdoor Theater productions.

"Now there's going to be another ingénue to take all the good roles," she said.

First off, I had no intention of bursting onto the community stage with any regularity. I really just wanted to make it through these twelve performances without missing any lines because I'm planning the next week's menu instead of staying in character. This woman had absolutely nothing to worry about.

My passion still eluded me.

In my continuing quest, I became a traveling kitchen gadget girl, hawking my wares in living rooms around Wichita County. I had never been to a Pampered Chef party when I called the 1-800 number to find a local contact, who showed up at my house within thirty minutes with a flyer and a spice packet. Two weeks later, I was demonstrating a recipe that required two bricks of cream cheese and half a dozen kitchen tools. I charmed the women in my living room enough to book my first few parties. From there, I was off with a tangible purpose and goals.

Trouble is I'm not much of a cook, mostly because I have issues with timers. I tend to burn things. When a recipe required a precooked pizza crust (aka flattened Pillsbury dough), I often pulled a blackened mess from the oven because I had been busy chatting up the guests. I was really good at the chatting part, and I loved meeting new people and seeing how they lived. The commission wasn't bad either. If I could make a hundred dollars for hanging out and drinking wine with a bunch of women, I could zest the lemons and crush the garlic to earn it. So what if I had to make a grocery run mid-party for a new tube of dough?

In order to make the most of my time in front of people, to get them to buy more and book more parties, I didn't wash the dishes from my cooking demo until I got home. I simply loaded them into the same plastic crate I'd used to cart them into the party. Later, in my own kitchen, at nine or ten at night, I'd wash the cream cheese residue and pick the garlic skins out of the crusher. This got old. And heavy. And less fun as I worked my way out of my circle of fun friends and into circles further and further away from people I actually wanted to hang out with.

I had a party scheduled for September 11th, 2001. When I called the hostess to reschedule, she thought that was silly. So, heavy of heart, I drove into the outlying areas beyond Wichita Falls. I followed the rural routes and two lane roads to a depressing little street of sad, run-down houses. I checked the address. Yes, this house, sorely in need of painting and mowing, the one with chickens in the yard, was where I'd spend the evening that the towers went down.

I did not have the energy to be my chipper self. I did not have the energy to pretend to the hostess that I was not angry that she made me drive all the way out here to her godforsaken hovel to fix her and her ONE GUEST a snack. I did not have the energy to ignore the hostess's hyper husband who was packing because he was a reservist who had just been activated.

I sure as hell did not have the energy to do the dishes. But I did, for another year. Then it was time to return to accounting. A friend from Junior League told me about an opening at her firm. Freemon, Shapard & Story—established, old school, and expensive. I figured with my Andersen background I'd fit right in. I dusted the lint off my best navy suit and picked up a pair of new pumps. I needed to rock the interview because, slight problem, I didn't have actual tax preparation skills. My tax knowledge was confined to stock options and spreadsheets. I did the complicated calculations and other staff completed the actual hands-on preparation. However, if I had learned nothing else during my consulting tenure, I had learned that anyone can be an expert, and it doesn't take long. I spent the entire interview stressing the transferability of my skills. There was no doubt in my mind I could prepare tax returns, so that's what I told the partners—over and over.

"I get it. You're very confident," one of them said. I'm pretty sure he just wanted me to stop talking.

I got the job.

On my first day, the same partner walked into my pretty office with the glass wall and inquired about my work ethic.

"When we give you tax returns to do, you're not going to let them pile up on your desk while you're looking at porn, right?"

We got along just fine.

Once again I was dressing up to go to work, spending three days a week at an orderly desk, drinking coffee, shuffling papers, and getting wicked fast at the ten-key. Life might not have been passionate, but it was good.

# God Bless Chuck E. Cheese's

❦

IF YOU HAVE CHILDREN, I have no doubt you have had to endure at least one visit to Chuck E. Cheese's. If not that particular rodent-themed chain, then another similar madhouse of chaos. I detested Chuck E. Cheese's, yet went there willingly, and often. It was better than the alternative: Staying home with the children. The Chuck E. Cheese's in Wichita Falls opened early some mornings for moms like me. We took our children there to climb on the toys in the cool air conditioning. Especially during the summer when, if you didn't get out before 7:00 am, it was already too hot to hit the playground.

The flashing lights and mind-numbing sounds of the indoor circus that is Chuck E. Cheese's were a small price to pay for an hour or two of air-conditioned activity that was not in your own living room. Seeing other moms was a bonus, sometimes. The tyranny of toddlers can transform the most interesting, attractive, and engaging women into blobs of half sentences and glazed eyes. And if I'm being honest, not every mother there was someone I would have chosen to spend time with were I not desperate for adult conversation. My standards might have suffered some.

The shitty pizza didn't help, but it sure went down easy.

One of the mornings I had resigned myself to the fate of Chuck E. Cheese's, I was pleasantly surprised to see a friend. Well, a friend of a friend really. Stephanie wasn't like us. She seemed better able to preserve her own life force in the midst of child-rearing. I wanted to be Stephanie. But even in my compromised state I knew that was weird and I didn't want her to know I was creepy like that.

I had met Stephanie at a Pampered Chef party and soon learned she was a writer. A real writer. Stephanie had studied journalism and written a novel. She kept journals. Now I did, too, in secret. Soon after meeting Stephanie, I had started scratching out my own thoughts into spiral notebooks between work at the accounting office, and making dinner while watching Oprah. Knowing Stephanie made writing seem like a real thing one could do, at least in private. I wondered if I could be a writer, too.

But that was crazy, right? Who is a writer?

I couldn't tell Stephanie. I couldn't tell anyone. Writing was a silly waste of time. It didn't seem like something normal people did. Being a writer seemed special, and I wasn't special. I didn't have anything to say, and I certainly didn't want to bother Stephanie or risk her thinking I was sucking up to her because she was special. Which she was because she was a writer. Obviously.

Textbook girl-crush.

But here she was, just another half-haggard mom at

Chuck E. Cheese's. There among the horns and the terrible music, standing next to the plastic rocking duck on the giant spring, occasionally reaching over without looking to right a falling child—ours or someone else's—and I suddenly felt courageous.

"I think um... I might want to try writing... a little," I managed to get out.

Stephanie's eyes lit up. "Do it!"

"You think?" I said.

"Yes, absolutely. Why not?"

Like writing was just an ordinary thing that any mere mortal could do.

"I really don't know how."

"Doesn't matter," she told me. "If you want to write, you just do it."

*Well, okay. If she says so.*

That was the moment equal parts of toddler diversion, enormous facsimile rats, and godawful pizza came together to give me exactly what I didn't know I needed. After that, everything poured out. I had found my writing angel and joined my first writing tribe. I was playing with terribly mixed metaphors. I read and wrote and joined Stephanie's writing group. I recited my work aloud in Stephanie's living room. It was awful; it was a start.

PART 2

# Where is Arkansas?

ॐ

I HAD JUST STARTED SETTLING in to my new life in Texas when my husband started asking what I thought about Arkansas.

*Excuse me, where?*

Because really, what does one think about Arkansas before one has actually been there? In my case, images of hillbillies living in something called a holler came to mind. I didn't think Bill Clinton or Walmart, and had no idea where Tyson chicken came from. To me, Arkansas was *Coal Miner's Daughter* meets a Steinbeck novel.

John said his company was considering building a plant in Rogers, Arkansas.

Why?

"To be near the chicken farms," he said.

Naturally.

Surely he wasn't suggesting we actually *go* to Arkansas. Hadn't I done enough? Hadn't I followed this man to the innards of Texas, settled into a canyon, and fought off scorpions and tarantulas using nothing but my bare hands and a few household utensils? I loved my husband, but I did not love him enough to entertain the thought of Arkansas.

*Remind me: Where is Arkansas, exactly?*

Texas was hot, dry, and ugly, but in my short time there I had learned it was also Texas—big with attitude and charm. What could Arkansas possibly have to offer?

*And where the hell was it, anyway?*

Wichita Falls wasn't exactly paradise. We had segregation, teen pregnancy, and the climate that turned any outdoor event—such as lunch on the deck or a walk around the neighborhood—into a painful and dangerous war with the elements. Did I really want my kids to be from this place? Settling in had taken a while, but now that I felt sane and secure in my new surroundings, I didn't want to give that up. After two years in Wichita Falls, I had a job I liked, a book club, and friends with whom I drank boxed wine on the driveway. What more could a girl want? I had found my people; therefore I was ready to dig into the hard clay soil and stay.

After casually dismissing John's silly requests for "thoughts about Arkansas," I forgot about any such place for several months. John didn't bring it up again until construction started on the new plant there. A couple of his work friends visited and interviewed for positions in Arkansas, then came back with reports that Rogers wasn't a bad place. They still needed an electrical engineer. John should check it out.

The stars must have aligned because after much dramatic sighing, I agreed to humor my husband of a decade by pretending I was willing to move to a place where corncob pipes were a thing. To my great surprise, I started to soften when I saw the town's website. First because they had a website—I'm easy that way—but also because Rogers, Arkansas, looked like a regular place with normal people who presumably attended school beyond the seventh grade. Rogers had trees, lakes, and temperatures that rarely topped 100 degrees. One could only assume the teen pregnancy rate was lower than that of Wichita Falls. I don't like to admit that all it took to sell me were a few well-framed shots at good angles and some decent Chamber of Commerce copy; I prefer to believe my better judgment favored the opportunity.

Two weeks later, we arrived in Arkansas for our house-hunting trip.

Five days after that, we made an offer on 3,000 square-feet of hardwood, crown molding, and granite countertops. The new adventure began.

In some ways, Texas had prepared me for Arkansas, but mostly I got a fresh hit of culture shock. That first year never could have convinced me that I would grow to love Arkansas, calling it home and fighting to keep it that way. I couldn't have known then that I would learn not only to identify Arkansas on a map, but to create real ties to that lopsided square in the middle of the country. Soon I would have answers to the question, *Where is Arkansas?*

Arkansas is where we would spend our tenth anniversary, and our twentieth.

Arkansas is where our children would learn to swim and bike and drive.

# Home Improvement Gone Wrong

ॐ

MY DAUGHTER AND I WERE standing at the kitchen table folding laundry when my husband sped past. In the moment it took me to look reach for an Aeropostale t-shirt, he was gone. Like the Road Runner. Meep, meep.

"I have never seen him move that fast," my daughter said.

Seconds later my son ran into the kitchen looking out the window after his father.

"What happened?" I asked.

"I don't know," he said. "All I heard was the drill, and then this really loud crash, and then like—water or something."

By the time my son finished reporting the facts, my husband was back, sweating and looking like Tom Hanks when Wilson died.

"Can you call the gas company?" he said, turning to run back up the hill of our backyard. And then, over his shoulder, an afterthought really, he said, "And get out of the house."

This could not be good.

I blew out the candles (no joke), grabbed my phone and eyed my MacBook on the kitchen counter. I decided to leave it. Surely, the situation wasn't that bad, right? I smelled gas, but my husband is handy. While I may have struggled with my roles in life, my husband has always known exactly who he is. And he is that guy, the one who fixes all the things, the guy who spends Saturday mornings at the home improvement store. John was not a guy who would blow up our house. So why had he been upstairs with a drill?

Recently, after a lot of misplaced hope that our air conditioner was "frozen up because of the heat," whatever that means, and a couple nights lying to the kids ("Yes, the air is on. Go to bed!") followed by a few more nights of letting them sleep downstairs, we replaced the unit. As I wrote the check, with barely enough room for all the words to name the amount, my husband told me the good news: "The downstairs unit will go next."

But what can you do? Since we were spending the cost of a used car on the A/C unit anyway, we decided to add on a humidifier. Surely the moistened air would pay for itself in avoided medical insurance copays related to croupy cough and eczema. But there was a problem. The crass A/C guys had the audacity to use a PVC pipe. Seriously, right? Who does that? Everybody KNOWS you use a copper pipe. Everyone knows that.

This inferior plumbing component kept my husband up at night. So first thing Saturday morning he headed off to Home Depot or Lowe's or wherever he goes on Saturday mornings, and came home with a tube of fine copper and a mission for the day. Home improvement is not mere puttering for John; it is meditation.

Or it was, until he drilled into that gas line.

Luckily, he knows not only where the gas main is, but also how to turn it off. Which is super handy, because it turns out the gas company's emergency line actually puts you on hold for a while before they tell you about the ONE GUY who is currently out on a call and will probably be there "pretty soon."

The gas man arrived within 30 minutes, cut off the gas to our house, and explained to my husband that he'd have to have the repairs made by a licensed plumber. After those were done, we were to call the gas company so they could come back and turn the gas back on.

"This is going to be expensive," my husband said.

I told him it was okay, because we were all alive. Plus, once you've bought an air conditioner, a plumber's bill seems like a bargain. "Such a stupid mistake," he said. "I can't believe I did that."

He's done worse. Once, while installing the backer board for a bathroom tile floor, he sawed through his thumb and then held it bleeding in the air until he finished the job. Because you don't slack off in the ER with a half-finished project waiting at home.

But this gas thing was easy, the only inconvenience being a few days without hot water and a stove. We played redneck—not showering and microwaving all our food.

"I learned one thing, that's for sure," John said after all was repaired and the contractor's bills had been paid.

"You have a gas leak, you do *not* call the gas company."

That's what he learned.

To be fair, I love the way John takes care of things around the house. If the occasional life-threatening mishap is the price we pay for his handiness, I'm okay with that. There's no ignoring that all the other wives want what I've got.

That's right: copper pipe.

# Writer Wannabe

❦

"I'M SORRY," said the elderly woman with just a hint of condescension. "Our group is only for *published* writers."

This after a full day lurking in the back of the room, observing the writers in their natural habitat at a day-long conference put on by a local writers group. I had searched all day for signs that any of these lucky people might join me in a writing group. How could this retired schoolteacher dismiss me so easily without even knowing that we were practically neighbors and I also love Barnes & Noble and I've done every single exercise in *The Artist's Way*?

The conference was my second attempt to find a group of Arkansas writers who would have me, or individuals I could convince to join me. Almost immediately upon arriving in town I had enrolled in a writers workshop at the local community college. When writers say it, *workshop* is just a fancy word for *class*—some writers still believe that *real* writing cannot be taught.

We met in a fluorescent-lit room to share our writing. I was the oldest student in a roomful of teens and twentysomethings. From our places at desks arranged in a U-shape in front of the teacher at the podium, we read our stories and poems aloud. Though brutal, those evenings with their angst, confusing peer critiques, and endless grabs for attention, kept me going in my strange new land. The workshop kept me writing, but I missed the tiny writing tribe I had joined in Texas. My fellow students weren't real writers, or even wannabes like me. They were just kids checking off a required course.

After the conference I returned to class, nursing the sting of rejection, a feeling I'd have to get used to as a writer. That night, the teacher mentioned his writing group. I seized the opportunity—possibly begging, certainly oozing desperation. Over the course of the next few weeks, my teacher brokered my acceptance to his group, which happened to be the same literary elites who had snubbed me at the conference. I showed them, quickly earning my place around the circle, despite my only professional writing experience: IRS letters and Junior League meeting agendas.

During the first couple of years at our Saturday morning Barnes & Noble meetings, I learned to tell a story, apply proper grammar, and send my words out into the world. Over and over and over. I scribbled in a lot of spiral notebooks. I wrote my first essays and got them published. I printed a stack of pages that I like to call my first novel, but which actually only amounted to 80,000 words loosely organized around a character who didn't really do anything or change much. Then one day I got a break in the strange new world called the Internet.

In 2007, after I'd been writing nearly every day for nearly three years, I got my first paid writing gig: Five dollars an article plus the promise of a share in ad revenue in exchange for 400 words, fifteen times a month. If you're good at math you'll realize that's $75. If that's not a motivator to create, you're just lazy.

"How are you going to come up with fifteen ideas every month?" my husband wanted to know.

Coming up with the ideas was not the problem. I delivered more than six hundred of them over the course of four years, and earned thousands of dollars in ad revenue in addition to that sweet $5 upfront payment. Soon I was the top ranked Google search result for "make a balloon arch" and "Halloween boo poems." People stopped me in the grocery store to tell me they were looking for this or that topic and there was my face on the screen. These were heady times indeed. Although the writing wasn't great, it got better over time. More importantly, I learned how to get the writing done, because you can't get fifteen articles completed without developing creative discipline. I climbed the clip ladder using my earliest writing to get better and better online gigs. Soon I was making $75 for one article, not fifteen of them. And then I got the call from WhoIsIsabella.com, a tiny startup with ambitions to be the women's MySpace. They wanted me to write whatever I wanted, for free, naturally, but still—whatever I wanted. Pretty soon, they offered me a monthly column, and with it, my first real excuse to say, "I'm on deadline," which is a fairly important milestone in any writer's career.

I needed a name for my column and struggled to find something that evoked my writing, which always seemed to center on the strange and occasionally beautiful moments in between celebrations, after the champagne has gone flat. That's where real life lives. My pragmatic side wanted something that started with the letter "A" because I remembered my mother teaching me how businesses used "A" names to get the best placement in the yellow pages. I figured this antiquated technology worked in the new online world, too, pushing "A" names to the top of all those blog rolls in websites' sidebars.

*After the Bubbly* was born.

I kept wearing out notebooks. I got a laptop so I could write from a lawn chair on the driveway while I watched the kids. And I got so published I would eventually leave my writing group because it cut into my writing time. Can't mess around when you're on deadline.

# Phases of Automotive Cleanliness

❦

NEW CARS ARE EXCITING, aren't they? You've got the shiny new paint job, all the exotic new sounds of blinkers and open door indicators, and of course that delicious new-car smell. You just know that this time is going to be different. This time you are going to maintain this nirvana of car interior forever. No more spilled coffee and fossilized fries. Because this car is the one, and you are more mature now. How hard could it be to keep a car clean, really? I mean, you're starting with a fresh canvas. You've been given a reset button and you are going to push that baby every week, at least.

That's phase one.

I entered this phase with a set of brushes and a microfiber duster. Two, actually—a big one for the exterior and a small one for the interior. Because dusting a car is normal new car behavior. Friends and neighbors mocked and told me it would never last. I showed them. Each week I diligently cleaned out the clutter, brushed all the nooks and cleaned out the crannies. I vacuumed, wiped, scrubbed and chamoised. Sometimes, at a stoplight, in what I now recognize as truly intervention-worthy behavior, I'd take the mini-duster out of the glove compartment and give the dash a wipe-down.

I'm not unique. Everyone keeps a new car clean for a certain period of time. The velocity of decay depends on many factors and applies not only to cars but to other things—clothing, jobs, relationships. These all start out new, become ever more comfortable, and then gradually, if we're not careful, decay into disrepair. I knew I was getting comfortable with the car when I realized it had been a month since I'd dusted the outside. I had collected too much stuff in the way-back to get into the compartment where I kept the duster. Hello, phase two.

In this season of our relationship, instead of dusting, I drove through the car wash, kept the inside relatively tidy, and even wiped down all the surfaces once a month. Sure, I'd lost the new car smell, but we were good together, the car and me. You could say we grew closer as I started to think of my car less as an orderly mode of transportation and started to treat it more like an extension of the house, where I could have a meal, get ready for work, and store those extra items that take up too much space in the closet. The comfortable phase wasn't so bad. Nobody got hurt. Everybody got to school on time. But once you settle into this phase, there's nowhere to go but into the pit of despair that is long-time car owner-ship: phase three.

In my case, the trouble started, as it often does, with coffee. The first few times I blotted it up and sprayed it down, returning the carpet to its original state. But over time I got over it. What's a little dried coffee next to all those junk food wrappers, after all? I was driving around town with an almost impressive accumulation of pencils, paper, string, gym clothes, individual shoes, and water bottles from 5Ks. And then the dog hair—lots and lots of dog hair—embedded in the carpet.

I reasoned the filth was not my fault because I was the one who took the kids to school and picked them up and fed them the occasional mobile meal and took the dog to the vet and therefore had to drink gallons of coffee to maintain the energy to do all this. My life, though figuratively ordered and relatively peaceful, was literally messy. And I had the car to prove it.

When it got really bad, I considered having the car detailed. But there was a problem. I would have had to clean it first. I could not let some guy who cleans cars all day—other people's cars, normal people's cars—know what a sordid slob I was. And the filth was nothing compared to the humiliating collection of CDs in the glove compartment, not to mention the fact that I still owned CDs. And then there was all the crap. Because who needs a storage unit when you've got a worn-in car? I carted around just-in-case umbrellas and blankets, sports equipment from sports my kids no longer played. There were grocery lists stuck to the seats with Jolly Ranchers, and in the center console was a five-year-old lip gloss and a pack of dry wet wipes. It was a time capsule of my life since the day I stopped caring about keeping the car clean.

I wanted to clean the car. I needed to clean the car. Every time I got in it, the car screamed failure.

*How hard could it be to keep a car clean?*

Really, really, really hard—no matter what the duster salesman tells you. Fortunately, there's a cure. For a low, low down and 60 easy payments, you can park a brand new clean canvas in your driveway for the neighbors to admire. Just know going in that its pristine beauty is fleeting. Adjust your expectations, because by the time you send in payment #36, you might just find a family of squirrels living under the seats. That's phase four.

# Timeline of Leaving the House for a Long Weekend

❦

REMEMBER WHEN WEEKEND getaways were easy? Spontaneous even? Come up with a great idea Friday morning, cut out of work early, throw a few things in the car, and hit the road. Enter two children and a dog and things get complicated.

Three weeks prior: Discuss ideal timing of weekend away and make official by sending spouse a digital calendar invite.

Night Before: Remain calm while spouse exhibits surprise that said weekend away is actually *this* weekend. Beg children to pack. Trade sleep for mild anxiety over all the things you could/would/should be doing instead of spending the weekend away.

Morning of: Remind spouse that weekend away actually begins in less than twelve hours.

Noon: Attempt accomplishing a weekend's worth of errands in a single lunch hour. Fail.

3:58 PM: Consider leaving work early, but decide it's better to stay after noticing that expression on your boss's face and remembering you have a mortgage.

5:15 PM: Leave work.

5:28 PM: Begin packing for long weekend, which begins four hours down the highway. What, the kids didn't pack last night, why should you?

5:31 PM: Remember that you do laundry on Sundays and therefore have no clean underwear to pack.

5:32 PM: Pack dirty underwear because luckily you're staying with family and can start a load when you get there.

5:47 PM: Start packing car. Argue about where the dog should sit.

5:59 PM: Finish packing.

6:02 PM: Look for snacks. Remember that you also shop for groceries on Sunday and therefore there are no snacks in the house.

6:03 PM: Discuss snack options that can be picked up on the way.

6:12: Get everyone in the car, including the dog, which will spend five hours at your daughter's feet because she lost this round to her brother in their sibling fairness algorithm that you will never fully understand.

6:14: Run back into the house for sweaters in case it gets chilly.

6:15: Look for car keys.

6:18: Pull out of the driveway.

6:19: Turn around to get the dog's leash.

6:22: Pull out of the neighborhood.

6:23: Ask your spouse if he/she remembered to close the garage door.

6:26: Close the garage door.

6:27: Ask one more time if we are sure we have everything. Get confirmation.

10:57: Arrive at destination.

11:13: Drive to Walgreen's to buy contact solution.

Midnight: Fall into a deep sleep, and dream about the

# We Used to Camp

☙

BEFORE OUR FIRST VISIT to an Arkansas state park, we had never seen a full-sized refrigerator at a campsite. And even though we are not adventurous campers, a satellite TV dish seems excessive for a trip to the lake. Still, to each their own. We have never roughed it in our lives, preferring to stock the car with good cheese and wine, packs of hot dogs and the makings of s'mores for one- or two-night exploits in the safely cultivated nature of state parks. These are typically filled with nice families and old people, often deserving to be called redneck, but only in the nicest way. Surely they were impressed with our four-man tent, Coleman cooler, and three different corkscrews.

Our move to "the Natural State" naturally spurred a renewed interest in camping. Arkansas had great parks, four seasons, and few, if any, scorpions, tarantulas, or rattlesnakes. We love the family bonding of camping and would do it more often if not for my incredibly rational fears. In addition to snakes, daddy longlegs, cuts, gashes, broken limbs, leeches, bears, poison ivy, The Itch, and past-its-prime potato salad, I also fear violent attackers. I just *know* something very bad is going to happen. Just because tragedy has not befallen us yet does not mean the day I dread is not coming. The signs are all there. Every camping trip follows the same pattern.

The evening starts out idyllic. Everyone is relaxed from a long day of fresh air and tubing or hiking or swimming. We sit around the campfire wiping marshmallow and chocolate off our faces like an ad for scouting. Our laughter mingles in the air with that of the other campers. Lightning bugs provide a magical ambiance. Cold beers and boxed wine go down easy. As the sky gets darker and the fire gets higher, the laughs get louder. Shrieks of children are replaced by cackles of old women as the grownups break out dirty stories, even though the kids can still hear them. Nobody cares because of the beverages. By now all is well with the world. I take my wined-up self to bed in the tent. The laughter dies off as others do the same, and I ponder the beauty of my life and the universe briefly before drifting off into a cricket-splendored sleep.

Almost.

Invariably, just as I'm drifting between conscious and not, I am jostled out of my blissful near-slumber by low-toned voices, steadily rising in increasing irritation, culminating in the following slurred retort:

"What's *that* supposed to mean?"

This is promptly followed by the slamming of a trailer door, or the crash of multiple aluminum cans, and then the squeal of tires.

Is it over? Sure. That mad guy went home, or to Sonic,

or to get more beer.

The fact that our fellow campers' conflict is done does not stop me from indulging a moderate panic attack. My mind reels to the only logical outcomes of such a situation: meth explosions, a B-grade horror film, and/or gunfire. Obviously, the disgruntled camper has abandoned the area only to retrieve ammunition at another location and return to settle the score. Perhaps an actual score—maybe a game of Yahtzee went bad. Nobody knows these things. All I know for sure is that we are defenseless in a tent while a madman is about. And you know madmen. If there's one, there are twenty, each with a unique and plausible motive to rape and kill us all, leaving our carcasses for the raccoons, and everyone knows they will eat anything. I console myself with one thought: Maybe, just maybe, the tire squealer is not a madman at all, but a regular terrified person just like me. He wouldn't think of messing with our tent without knowing what we're concealing and carrying, right?

After a while, the hum of the refrigerator lulls me to sleep.

Maybe next time we rig up a TV.

# Spray Tanning

❦

I HAD A TAN ONCE. I was 17, trading my labor for carcinogens at Tahitian Tan. One night a week and Sunday afternoons, my best friend and I checked other tanners in and out, marked their cards, and cleaned out the beds between customers. Then we locked the doors and spent as long as we wanted lying on Plexiglas, surrounded by fake sunlight that would bestow upon us an artificial glow. Soon, my naturally fair skin turned a strange umber color. To enhance the effect, I wore a flat whitish pink lipstick, which made me look like a negative. Upping the tacky ante, I applied a tri-colored blue/silver/pink eye shadow treatment. When I started adding frosted lip gloss, I had to be stopped. An intervention was staged and I soon left the tanning salon for part-time work with fewer health hazards.

That was a long time ago, and I haven't achieved any amount of "color" since then. But a trip to Mexico—and a conveniently timed Living Social offer—took me to a tanning salon for the first time in more than two decades. But this time I'd be smart. This time I would not subject my body to damaging light rays, but rather opt for a paint job to simulate tan skin.

The girl working the registration desk at the tanning salon was not particularly tan. She checked me in and offered me an add-on primer, which is something that will be sprayed on me before the solution that "tans" my skin, aka paint. The girl highly recommended the primer. In fact, if I didn't get the pre-treatment, I was wasting my time, she said. I didn't tell her that I wasn't planning to do this again, that I was only there because I wanted to look good on my vacation, or at least the first day of it, before the sand and water scrubbed off my "tan." I agreed to the extra $8 for the premium treatment, figuring it was like occasionally adding on that extra presoak at the car wash. You don't actually know that it makes a difference, but you don't actually know that it doesn't either, and so you bet on optimism. Just this once, anyway. You're not even paying for the actual thing as much as for the right to believe it works because you paid for it.

The front desk girl walked me down a long hall with doors on either side that had the tanning bed glow coming out from under them. I remembered these rooms from my Tahitian Tan days. I remembered the little eye goggles, the hum of the beds, the warmth of the plastic, the claustrophobic feeling of the top of the bed coming down on me, and the shock of dark and quiet as the timer went out. Once we had passed all the rooms, she took me down another hallway to a room with what she called a bed, but was actually a large booth, the kind TSA might use to see my skeleton.

In this room I learned to clean my face and my hair with

wet wipes and how to pull my ears out of the hairnet so that they would get painted—I mean *tanned*—too. She gave me two pieces of cardboard, which she referred to as slippers, and told me to peel the protective paper off and stick these slippers onto my feet. Finally, she demonstrated with great detail how to pump five pumps—not four, not six, but five pumps—of lotion from the dispenser on the wall onto my hands and rub it in all over my hands. Then I was to pump again and only rub the lotion onto my palms. So, to recap, that's cleansing, hairnet, ears, slippers, and a precisely measured lotion application technique. This was becoming a lot of work already, and that was the easy part. Next I had to get in the bed.

The attendant demonstrated the very specific positions I needed to assume in order to get a good tan. If I didn't get these right, the spray paint would not be applied evenly, to say nothing of the primer. The first couple of positions were fairly straightforward: facing the front, facing the back. Just when I started congratulating myself for being such a quick study, we moved on to proper side body positioning. My instructor, in what has surely become a body of knowledge worthy of some type of continuing education credit, was extremely specific about how my arms needed to line up with the sides of the machine. I was to angle my hands just so and then bend my wrists in an unnatural way. I felt like I was back in the '80s again, not at the tanning salon, but in a Bananarama video. At the same time, I actually had to operate the machine.

*Push the button, face front, get sprayed, face back, get*

*sprayed, face front, blow-dry, repeat, walk like an Egyptian, spray, blow, repeat, done.*

I was confused, yet hopeful.

Before she left, the attendant tried to reassure me with her reminder that the magic tanning booth is voice activated. By that she actually means that the booth will tell me what to do. Then she left me alone with the Transformer machine. I got undressed and put on the hairnet. I started the lotion routine while reminding myself of the ratio. *Five to one, five to one, five to one. I can do this.* But after one pump I realized I wasn't going to be able to put the cardboard slippers on with slippery hands so I stopped to stick on the foot-shaped pieces of cardboard. I resumed five pumps of lotion. *Was it five including the one for the palms or was it five PLUS the one for the palms?* I panicked, realizing I was rubbing the lotion up onto my wrist—like any sane person would do if they had five pumps of lotion all over their hands—and then I wondered if my wrists would end up tragically white.

I stepped into the bed and pushed the green button as I'd been instructed. When the spray hit I wondered if I was supposed to close my eyes or hold my breath. I quickly closed my eyes as the spray passed over my face. So far I felt like I was my Toyota at the drive-through car wash and this paint and/or primer was that pretty multicolored soap. Then I realized I was scrunching up my face, which probably just painted every expression line I have right into my "tan."

Everything went as well as could be expected until it was time to turn to the side. The girl had been adamant that my toes butt right up against the line, but not over it.

"Whatever you do, don't put your toes over the red line," she had warned.

In fact, everything she had said about the sideways experience had seemed ominous.

"If you don't get the sides right, it's just going to look... weird."

As if standing in a tanning machine, looking at my naked self in a full-length mirror was anything less than weird. Still, I was committed at this point, and I did all right until it was time for the blow-dry. Again, just like the car wash. I did something wrong, which prevented the right side of my body from drying properly. I waited a minute before getting dressed and admired my amber glow in the full-length mirror. I was enjoying the moment when the "bed," aka the standing shower stall, started to clean itself. The water rolled down the walls of the spray paint bed. Magical. That would have been a handy feature back in my Tahitian Tan days. I'd have had so much more time for tanning if I hadn't had to waste it cleaning the beds.

I wonder what Then Me would have thought of Now Me. Would Then Me have been disappointed, hoping Grown-Up Me would have been more secure? Or would I have been shocked that the over-40 me cared about looks at all? I'm not sure my younger self would be too proud, which is fine, as long as she doesn't figure out the truth—that we're all somewhat stuck, caught between adolescence and young adulthood. Past 20 we don't change much on the inside. The experiences add up, but at our core we're just insecure teenagers trying to fit in and make our way. She's too young to know all that. Let her keep her innocence a little longer.

The result of my 2014 tan was only slightly less ridiculous than the 1987 version, but that's okay. I'm an adult now. I can afford the $30 tan extender lotion, and the new sheets I needed to buy when my paint job stained them.

# Another City, Another Tax Department

꩜

AFTER ARRIVING IN ARKANSAS, the first thing I did after settling into a writing group was get a part-time job at an accounting firm. When the Arkansas firm called my old boss from Wichita Falls, the reference consisted of, "You'd better bag her up right now." And with that glowing recommendation, I was once again gainfully employed—at least between the hours of 9 and 3. The tax department was where all mommy CPAs went to die—or cultivate solid, predictable careers, depending on your perspective. Having a job with the lowest possible stress level (tax accountant) for a very low-stress employer (small-town accounting firm) should not have been stressful, especially considering I was only working two days a week. Somehow I managed to court constant anxiety around quitting time. I couldn't quite seem to get out of each day with enough cushion to make it home for the school bus or the end of preschool.

Summertime childcare was a problem. Had we been better Christians, I could have worked the Vacation Bible School system for an entire summer's worth of free babysitting. However, we heathens had to pay for professional sitters, or at least willing teenagers with reliable transportation. After weeks of begging around, I finally got the number of someone "wonderful." On her second day, she took my 4- and 6-year-old children to her house, where there was the lethal object feared by over-protective and regular moms alike: a swimming pool.

"They were bored," she said. Oh, the judgment.

"What did you use for car seats?" I asked. I knew the car seats were in my car, where they belonged, because automotive transportation of the most important humans in the world was not on my list of duties to delegate to a teenage girl.

She shifted in place.

"What about life jackets?" I asked. "You know they can't swim, right?"

"Oh, yes!" She looked excited to have the right answer. "My parents have tons of life jackets."

Aha, the parents, who my children spent the day with. I'm sure they were very nice people, but they also could have been into drugs or human trafficking, or just really liberal with processed snacks. You can't expose your kids to just anyone. So, no, sweet misguided girl, you won't be coming back.

Without a sitter, the kids spent the rest of my summer working days at the neighbor's house, who I paid in cash and value-sized boxes of Goldfish.

Besides the stress, which I wouldn't have been able to avoid anywhere, and the childcare woes, the job itself wasn't exactly dreamy. The guy I worked with every day liked to hang around my office, slowly telling stories about the firm, the clients, the town, or the latest thing he had seen on Waste-SomeTime.com. I tried to be nice, because he was, in a way, my boss. But mostly I had to learn to deal with him because he was just there, too often, leaning on the door jamb. After the first few weeks, I realized that if I wanted to get my work done so I could jet out the door at 3 o'clock to pick up the kids, I'd have to start training Waste Some Time Guy. Each time he showed up, I gave him less and less attention. Eventually, I could get away with only a slight pause to acknowledge his presence before getting back to entering data.

My second year at the firm was Waste Some Time Guy's tenth, and the year the partners finally promoted him to manager. In the big firms, if you weren't offered this title after five years, it meant the partners wanted you to leave. But this was a small firm in a small town and Waste Some Time Guy was a damn fine tax accountant. Still, ten years. I couldn't picture myself doing the same work for a few years, much less a decade. Waste Some Time Guy could knock out some returns, but he wasn't great with the people parts of his job. Enter one ambitious mommy-tracked firecracker who can not only attack a pile of returns in a single bound, but also train new staff, manage their work load, draft a letter to the IRS, and write articles for the annual Board of Accountancy newspaper feature.

Added bonus: She's part-time, so she would never have to be promoted!

By tax season, I had taken up residence in the junior

staff war room so they could have immediate access to me at all times. One March afternoon, as I reached for the next folder that held the next trust return on my schedule, the one I had prepared on this very date the year before, it struck me that at this rate I'd be sitting in this precise spot next year, too, answering the same newbie questions, preparing the same tax return for the same client on the same day for roughly the same pay. All I'd have to look forward to would be Waste Some Time Guy's stories.

There had to be a better way. Surely, this ten-keyed existence wasn't the purpose of my life. There was only one way to find out. Once tax season was over, I said goodbye to Waste Some Time Guy and the college kids, and went home to write.

# Home Party

❦

I HAD NOT CHANGED into a cute outfit, reapplied my makeup, or blown out my hair. That was my first mistake. Thinking I belonged at my neighbor's party was the second. Within one minute of my arrival I was handed a glass of Chardonnay. In the marble tiled kitchen, over artichoke dip and four flavors of cookies, my neighbor introduced me to the usual suspects: Matchy-Matchy Mom, Sweet Preggers, Bawdy Betty, and a cluster of women whose occupation was maintaining their ideal underweight and festive seasonal decorating. Off to the side, clear of the dips and "white death," stood the Pilates Instructor. Stunning, with symmetrical features, dark skin, raven hair, and beautiful breasts I could not help but admire because they were not only prominently featured in a low-cut lace-up blouse, but also the primary topic of conversation—where she'd gotten them, how much she'd paid, how she'd had to buy an entire new wardrobe to accommodate them, et cetera.

We were invited to shop for overpriced costume jewelry from my neighbor's friend, who would endure in this business for five parties or until her friends owned everything in the catalog, whichever came first. I knew because I had logged my own hours in the home party business, first pushing kitchen gadgets for Pampered Chef and then home décor with Southern Living, despite the fact that I am far from culinary and even further from any kind of Southern sense of decor. But it's rude to decline an invitation to sit on the other side of the pitch, and this party came with plenty of wine.

I tried to be a good guest. I complimented Sweet Preggers on her perfect basketball belly, had the requisite discussions about children and teachers and cell phones for sixth graders, and tried not to notice the size of the diamonds or speculate on which were actually CZs and which were real enough to burden their owners in debt better invested in real estate, education, or plastic surgery. In short, I tried to deny my delightfully judgmental nature. I tried on jewelry and accepted instructions on how train my help. I had fun.

As the wine continued to flow, the stories got better. I inhaled tales of escortish employment, tragic Brazilians (the salon treatments, not the people), where to get Botox for ten dollars a unit, which husbands couldn't get it up anymore, and—in a related story—which wives took entirely too many tennis lessons, yet never seemed to get any better. One particular hot mess of a gorgeous blonde told me she was from Greenville, South Carolina, which used to be nice but isn't anymore.

"It's full of Northerners," she said.

Pity.

More wine and we ditched the ladylike portioning of artichokes and cheese, digging into the buttery casserole dish with water crackers.

"I don't need this," one lovely anorexic said.

*You do*, I thought, eyeing her veiny, fuzz-covered arms.

Then the drunken Pilates instructor decided I was in need of conversion. She cornered me, drew me away from the others and told me how she'd get me on a "clean diet," break me of my "sugar addiction."

"No thanks," I told her.

She pointed a bony finger up and down my body. "You're fine, you're tiny," she said, as if I had requested her assessment. "But I'll tell you what your problem is: You don't sleep at night."

This was news to me.

"I sleep fine," I said, smiling and looking for a way out.

"But you don't have energy," she continued. "You don't sleep and you have low energy."

I laughed. "No, I feel pretty good. Really. But, thank you." I turned toward the cookies.

"I can tell by looking at you." She leaned back and said, without flinching, "It's those dark circles under your eyes."

I wish my mind worked faster, offering up a clever comeback on cue. But it doesn't. I jokingly blamed my sleepy look on age, to which Pilates responded that age was nothing but a number and that our bodies are temples. Hers apparently a shrine to liquid plastic.

I escaped to join the women at the appetizer trough. Under the influence, they had become even raunchier. Positions were compared. Affairs were catalogued. Names were named. All in all, a good time. At the end of the evening, I picked out a very nice pretend diamond tennis bracelet and handed my card over to the sales rep. As I was leaving, my neighbor invited me to Girls' Nights Out at "the club." I said I'd check my calendar, but I wouldn't. I'd rather stay home with my quaint lack of cleavage and the budding lines between my eyebrows, with my own wine and cheese. Something told me if I spent too much time with these women I wouldn't be able to sleep at night.

# That One Time I Was Adulterous

✦

IT STARTED OUT INNOCENTLY ENOUGH, as these things often do. Just a text here, some slight dissatisfaction there. There was no big conflict, but rather a slow growing apart that snuck up on me. Everything became inconvenient. Nothing personal, but I had needs and he was no longer able to meet them. We had been together nearly ten years, almost half my adult life with the same man. He knew how to make me feel beautiful. But the idea of someone new, with new techniques, thrilled me and at the same time it made me feel guilty as hell. Before I knew it I was trapped in the throes of an adulterous relationship.

My friends were no help. They actually encouraged the betrayal. What's the big deal? They wanted to know. You need to do what works for you, Lela. And on one level, I knew they were right. I knew my relationship was over, but I clung to it, and in the clinging only hurt myself. I could see it in the mirror. Slowly, guiltily, I exchanged furtive texts with a stranger and, along with them, a troubling internal dialogue.

*When could we meet?*

*Was I really ready for this?*
*Had I already crossed a line?*

But in another town, another county, surely, I could keep this a secret. And who would blame me? It's not like I'd gone looking for someone new, but I hadn't guarded against this either. I had let things go too long.

So here I was, meeting in secret. We were awkward together. After all those years, to feel the touch of another, hands through my hair. After all those years, it felt scary and exciting. How could he possibly know what I liked? I soaked in the thrill of the moment while trying not to think about how I might feel the next morning. Would I regret my reckless behavior or was this the start of a new long-lasting relationship?

In the six months before I strayed, we had only "been together" once. I blamed myself. I'd gotten busy, couldn't make time for him. But he had to take some of the blame. He wasn't as attentive as he had been earlier in our relationship. He didn't seem to listen to me anymore, or remember what was important to me. And then there was that spat. We'd had an agreement. He had vowed to protect me from myself. No matter how I begged or what celebrity resuscitated their style stature, he was never, *ever* to give me bangs.

And then one day, bangs.

Followed by his callous refusal to take responsibility for my actions.

That hurt, but I forgave him. So much history, after all. But we were never the same after that. Now, in the hands of another man, I'm torn between two blowouts, breaking all the rules. I don't know if I'm ready for a full confession, a reckoning. All I know is I can't go on like this. I can't have it both ways.

Who would want two hairdressers, anyway?

# A Simple Plan

☙

AT A RECENT DINNER with girlfriends I learned a shocking truth: 90% of them fantasize about murdering their husbands. I'm not talking about passive, "what if he fell off the ladder" daydreams such as those I occasionally indulge. I'm talking full-on deliberate master planning of the demise and dispatch of the spousal body. Maybe because most of the women I know are the primary food and personal grooming product providers for their husbands, most of the strategies involve some sort of poisoning. Most imaginative method: Arsenic injected into a tube of toothpaste.

Before that night with the girls, and aside from my idle musings on what my life might look like sans spouse, I'd never given actual murder much thought. After that night, I started to wonder: Was I irresponsible to *not* have a plan? Everybody else had one. What was wrong with me? What if I suddenly met a hot pool boy or a lonely underwear model? Didn't I owe it to myself to plan for any and all contingencies? Having an exit strategy is always comforting and comfort makes me happy. Since we all know that when mama's not happy, ain't nobody happy, I quickly reasoned that when mama has a murder plan, she could get downright delirious.

That's called selfless mothering.

So I set out to formulate a plan. I did not want to copy any of my friends' plans because that's not ethical. Plus, they would know the details of my plan and you never know when a friendship can sour. Here in the suburbs we are one silent auction gone wrong from a grudge that can last for generations. I had to be original.

I pondered for days. At the grocery store and in carpool line I would try to dream up ways to off my faithful husband. Nothing came. It might have helped if I were angry or if he had done something awful. But he wouldn't. Still, I needed a plan. This wasn't personal; it was practical. I had nearly given up on my ability to accomplish a simple task when, over chips and salsa at our favorite Mexican restaurant, it hit me. My husband reached into the basket for the last of the chip shards while simultaneously declaring, "All right, that's it, no more chips!"

The kids and I rolled our eyes knowing two things. One, there would be more chips and he would eat them. We all would. And two, only my husband would later complain that "something didn't agree" with him.

*Perhaps it was the bushel of fried cornmeal, dear.*

When indulging in Mexican food, it is critical to know one's limits. This knowledge is honed over a lifetime of enchiladas and chimichangas. Just as young people learn their tolerance to alcohol by trial and error, so too must the Mexican-food aficionado learn the appropriate balance between too much and not enough. My husband has not mastered this critical life skill. He habitually orders the Grande, the Gordo, the Mucho Dos Fried Platter. And he eats it—all of it. With chips and beer.

The last time we had Mexican, he swore he felt his heart quivering around in his chest.

My husband's failure to moderate his intake is the reason we have never eaten Mexican food for lunch. It is why we only go out for Mexican food once or twice a month, even though it is our favorite food. It is why he does not eat for twenty hours after any documented Mexican Food Incident (MFI). His lack of restraint is also the way I will kill him one day, if he crosses me. Or if that pool boy opportunity pans out.

All I have to do is ply my husband with chips and guacamole and fajitas smothered in queso.

I'll start slow so he doesn't realize what I'm up to. Once a week. Twice. Thrice. Until one day he keels over in pain as his insides explode, piñata-like, all over the fake terra cotta floor in a final, fatal MFI.

In his final moments, I will offer comfort. He will pull me in close, stroke my face, and utter his last words.

"That's it," he'll squeak. "No more chips."

# Why I Don't Have Tattoos

❦

AS I ORDERED MY TALL drip medium roast, I couldn't help but notice the cute barista's impressive inked sleeve of fish and lyrics. Because I'm middle-aged and needle-averse, the only thing I could think of to say was, "Didn't that hurt?"

"Not really," he said as everyone does, unless they are trying to impress you with how much pain they endured by choosing to have a certain body part tattooed.

"Do you have any tattoos?" he asked.

I shook my head and stared in disbelief.

"Not even one? Seriously?"

What's hard for me to believe is that my lack of tattoos is hard for a millennial to believe, but we're the minority now. We, the un-inked, are boring, uncreative, and lacking in color.

Under the influence to my otherwise liberal father's consistent and strongly worded disapproval of tattoos, I developed my own feelings about permanent ink. I failed to consider them an option, mostly because when I came of age in the '80s, tattoos were for only bikers, ex-cons, gang members, carneys, and really edgy guys in rock bands. Maybe, *maybe*, for girls who grew up in a commune—of bikers. When my best friend got one on her upper thigh, it was definitely scandalous. But she was cool in a way I never could be. Surely tattoos would not infiltrate the ranks of regular people like me.

Certain fraternities started encouraging their brothers to pledge lifelong association with ink. Next, naturally, came sorority girls and their cute ankle dolphins. I was on my way to a solid career in accounting before I saw one of those, and it was obscured by pantyhose. The next tattoo I saw on someone I knew was my colleague at my first professional job at the big accounting firm. She showed me a dainty frog on her hip, almost always covered up by her underwear or a bathing suit. That ink was for the eyes of intimate partners only, or a friend in a bathroom stall of a Mexican restaurant.

More than any cultural norms or parental influence, I've stayed inkless all these years because of my fear of commitment. How does one select a decoration forever, anyway? I can't even wear the same shirt for an entire day. I certainly can't choose a symbol or sentiment I'd want to live with forever. I have been married more than twenty years now, and raised two children to healthy teenager-hood. That's commitment enough. So when it comes to churches, charitable causes, and tattoos, I am unwilling to go all in. I'm not flighty; I've simply used up my capacity for commitment on other things.

On one hand, I admire people who have tattoos. I understand when you want to commit to a certain idea forever. Maybe tattoos are the ultimate accountability, keeping the inked forever tied to their momentary commitment. Once you've got the tattoo, you're in. On the other hand, I don't really see the point. A friend of mine recently got an acorn on her wrist. She's in her late 30s. She's coming into her own, getting comfortable in her skin. I get that, but forever the acorn, never the oak? I know another guy who got angel wings spanning his back when his daughter was born. Nice sentiment, but I wanted to know what sort of placement Child #2 receives and if he's thought through the psychological ramifications of that. My neighbor got a colorful fairy permanently affixed to his bicep just after he turned 50, and just before he got a divorce. I don't get that. Also, what's up with stars?

I remember my brother arguing with my dad about the merits of ink, using some old guy he knew as evidence.

"He still really likes his tattoo," my brother said.

"What else can he say?" my dad answered.

Nailed it.

So, yes, I'm a minority here in the new millennium, marked only by a C-section scar, an old small pox vaccination, and more freckles than are necessary. Not getting a tattoo is a commitment in itself. I'm forever doomed to be seen as a novelty by baristas everywhere.

"Don't you regret never getting one?" I imagine some nurse's aide asking me one day.

"Nope," I'll respond. "I still really like my unpainted skin."

Because at that point, what else can I say?

# Not Much for Christmas

☙

I DON'T NEED MUCH for Christmas, really. Just family and togetherness is all it takes to make me feel content at the holidays. I'm happy as an elf in felt as long as our little family is safe and snug together, with a ham in the oven, some carols on the stereo, and a few pine boughs cut from the tree out back. Those reminders of our good fortune at this blessed time of year—that's all I really want.

That said, once the tree has been trimmed, the nog has been drunk, and the children have been nestled all snug in their beds, I can't help but feel we're not really doing Christmas right. It's like Christmas doesn't ever really *feel* like Christmas, not like a real Christmas, a December flyer, late-year rom-com, miracle at the end of my cul-de-sac kind of Christmas. That kind of magic is missing every single year.

Don't get me wrong, I'm not complaining.

It's just that a decent tree would be nice, one with ornaments that don't look like they've been collected from the clearance bin at Yule-Mart. (Those discount lights can deliver quite a shock if you're not careful.) Holiday décor need not be fancy. Who wants to fuss with matching stockings, anyway? Not me. I'm happy to sit in the glow of the gas hearth and watch a good old-fashioned Christmas movie. But please, nothing with children. As if they don't suck enough life out of the season without casting them in some heartrending yarn. Does anyone care if Timmy's Christmas wishes come true?

Snowmen are also overplayed, in my humble opinion.

As for gifts, well, you know me. I don't need anything. I've got everything I need right here. I have my health and my happy little family, and the broken angel and the plastic wreath. What earthly delight could add to this bounty of opulence? What material object could possibly increase my overwhelming joy?

However, if I give *you* a gift, feel free to gush. Because 'tis better to give than to receive and I do enjoy giving. So when I have pondered and shopped and wrapped and waited with bated breath for you to open a gift, please dial up the jolly. If anyone wanted to express his or her fondness for me in a token gift, please note that I have plenty of slippers and Mango Sunset body butter. With thoughtful gift in hand, one's thoughts naturally turn to wrapping. On this topic I offer this simple advice: gift-wrapped. Decorative bags, no matter how festive, are the lazy gifter's choice. Can you picture the three wise men carrying bags with tissue paper into the barn to greet the baby Jesus? Failure to properly wrap a gift announces to the world that you are not mentally competent enough to master the rigors of Scotch tape.

Joy to the world, indeed.

You know what else I'd like at Christmas? A little romance, damn it. I've seen the movies. I know someone out there is getting swooped into a carriage for a ride around the frosted wonderland of Central Park. I know someone this very Christmas is reuniting with their one great and true love, who also happens to be a millionaire who loves dogs. I know there is a woman receiving a surprise ten-carat diamond after being serenaded by Sting and The Rockettes.

While we're wishing, I don't understand why it can't snow on Christmas. Every Christmas. Or was Bing Crosby just trying to torture us with inflated expectations? You know what else might really give me that Christmas feeling once and for all? Santa. Just once I'd like to see that guy at my door with an oversized check ala Publisher's Clearinghouse so I can pay off all those credit cards come January.

That would be super Christmasey.

Like I said, I don't need much. I'm just asking that we all try just a little bit harder to usher in the season of joy.

# Smudging Optional

⊙ঠ

THE WORD "RELEASE" in the headline should have tipped me off. As in *13 Ways to Release 2013*. But how could the article, written by a perky blond life coach, be anything but deeply enlightening? Release 2013. Let it go, mindfully, intentionally, with gratitude. And if all that doesn't work, special pricing for one-on-one coaching.

I couldn't help but click. As one does during the first week of January, I had been eating right, replacing evil incandescent bulbs with LED, and organizing closets as if the fate of Earth depended upon my ability to locate a single set of matching sheets on command. I was ready, desperate even, to get rid of the old and usher in the new. Be gone, old nasty. Bring on the glistening fresh 2014.

I was curious, too. How does one shed last year? Isn't it already gone? But I felt confident the wise one knew some secret magic for saying a permanent farewell to 2013. And of course by "magic" I mean "concrete advice that could be accomplished without using my credit card or a hiring a domestic staff."

I had to know.

At first skim, the oracle's advice looked promising. Much of it consisted of making lists of different types, and then accepting, celebrating, or burning said lists. (Ritualistic dancing optional.) Lists I can do. Lists are my oxygen. Lists are humanity's greatest technological feat. And burning stuff is fun. So far, we're all winning.

From there, however, our fearless leader's tips became increasing less illuminating. There was some vague advice to "feel grateful," followed by a suggestion that we might quite literally wash away the past year with a salt bath. No offense to the wise one, but I prefer a salty martini.

I read further with the beginnings of an eye-roll forming on my I'm-cynical-because-I'm-alive face when our resident fount of wisdom blasted my optimism into a pile of lifeless fairy dust. The pinnacle of her system, after I had presumably made my lists and lit them on fire while feeling grateful in a salty tub, was to "smudge" my home.

Call me an overachiever, but at this point—with one husband, two teenagers, a dog, the occasional uninvited pest, and a seasonal aversion to cleaning products—my home is already quite adequately smudged. The last thing I need is more mud on the floor and makeup on the countertops. Not to mention whatever keeps causing my dog to drag her ass across the carpet.

But this wasn't what our guru was talking about. Sadly, she was also not referring to any kind of eyeliner, which is unfortunate because a trip to Sephora is always cause for celebration. And I could have made a list. There's not much in this world that can't be improved with plumping lip gloss, black eyeliner, and a steady hand.

The smudging our authority suggested was the ancient practice of bundling sage or other herbs, lighting them afire, and using the resulting smoke to purify the area (or aura) of any negative energy, bad feelings, yucky thoughts, or wayward spirits. For centuries, respected religions and native peoples around the world have practiced some form of smudging, which is pretty amazing when you consider that they didn't even have the Internet to teach them how to do it. And smudging is just one way to release the year gone by. How primitive cultures ever figured out the other twelve without the aid of Wi-Fi and broadband is inconceivable.

Unlike practitioners of olde—who I imagine gathered their herbs mindfully, in a sacred place, perhaps on a day ordained by one god or another—the modern medicine woman has to remove her negative energy in between work, school, mani-pedis, and catching up on "Downton Abbey." Lucky for her, a two-pack of smudge sticks goes for less than seven dollars on Amazon. (Who said that Prime account wouldn't pay for itself?) Or, if she's more committed to the lifestyle, she can pick up her sticks from the Shaman's Market, a highly reputable online retailer that reminds customers that "smudges put out a lot of soothing smoke."

*Soothing*, said no evil spirit ever.

Pre-Internet, in a faraway land called the West Coast, I witnessed plenty of smudging, mostly practiced by people next to me at outdoor concerts. Oh, the sage I've inhaled and the floaty-dancing I've observed. In hindsight, perhaps I was the evil spirit these liberated souls were attempting to purge. We'll never know for sure. All I'm certain of is that, unfortunately, the poultry seasoning high does nothing for me. So, enticing as the idea of lighting yet another thing on fire in service of clearing out the old, smudging probably wasn't for me. I'm not native peoples. And I'm not a girl in a flowing skirt and a halter-top. By the looks of it, neither was our coach.

So, why?

Why had she embraced smudging? Was it simply another bullet point to round out the article? No one could blame her for that. But why not, "Light a candle from Bath and Body Works"? That might have been more on-brand.

I'm no coach in the game of life, but I say release all you want, make the lists, clean out the cupboards, drink the kale juice, but leave the smudging to professionals. Most of us have no business burning herbs for bad-mojo-removal's sake. That goes double for accountants, engineers, people who would ever precede "smudged" with a hashtag, and anyone with an asymmetrical bob.

Sorry, coach, I'm sitting this one out.

# We Are Dog Park Villains

☙

MY DOG LIBBY is the Cutest Dog Ever. We rescued her from a local animal shelter. She likes birds, squirrels, sticks, and walks. One weekend, we decided to take her on a real nature walk because we're hardcore hikers, or maybe because we found an easy trail that was well-maintained and located in a town where the average age of "hikers" is 75. The outing went so well that we decided afterward to take Libby to the dog park.

"Are you sure this is going to be okay?" asked my husband.

"Please. It's a *dog* park."

"You don't think she could get in a fight or anything?"

"Oh. My. God. Let's go. Nothing is going to happen."

The five of us—Libby, the kids, my husband, and me—walked by the dog park toward the double-gated entrance, watching all the cute doggies frolic and anticipating our Libby joining them in pure canine glee. We got to the gate all smiles and waggy tail. What you're supposed to do is enter through the first gate, then close it before entering into the second gate so that no dogs escape. Nobody had to tell us that.

However, the *very* excited (presumably male) dogs on the other end of the gate were waiting for their moment, had been waiting it seemed for days—maybe weeks—for just such an opportunity. Before we could get the first gate closed, three dogs jumped up, pushed down the latch, and escaped onto the wilds of the adjacent bike trail in hot pursuit of our now terrified Libby.

Just as my husband was chastising our son for opening the gate—because let's face it, we are a family who likes to assign blame as soon as possible and apologize later—a very excitable Dog Mama started to lose it. She came at us in a rage. "My dog won't come back!"

I understood how she felt. Our first family pet was an Italian Greyhound who often took off at warp speed out the front door. Simon caused me to spend many an evening driving the neighborhoods around our house coaxing him into the car with a piece of bacon and the assistance of kind strangers. In this situation, Simon would have been in the next state by the time we realized he had fled. Runaway dogs are stressful. I get it. But still, lady, have a Xanax.

I was unstressed because I knew Libby would not go far. She's a cowerer. Soon enough, my son had caught up to the pack and held her by the collar. We got her back on the leash, the woman stopped freaking out, and the Davidsons enjoyed a little time inside the safe confines of the dog park, trying and failing to make dog family friends. All's well that ends well.

As we walked away, my daughter turned to me and said,

"We're the bad people at the dog park, aren't we?"

Yes, dear daughter. Get used to it. We are the antiheroes of Dog Paradise. When we arrive in the future, we'll be greeted with sighs and eye-rolls. People will mutter under their breath. "It's *those* people."

*Blacklisted from the Dog Park*. I smell an anthology.

Oh, wait, that's just Libby.

# Rock the Bikini

☙

IT WAS FEBRUARY. I didn't want a bathing suit, but I needed one. My husband and I were going to Mexico to celebrate twenty years of home and kids and fighting about the silverware drawer. So I was shopping for a bathing suit on my phone. I clicked tiny images of anorexic-looking Asian girls in swimsuits constructed from less fabric than your average ankle sock. Faced with all that taut young skin, I couldn't help but picture my own abdominal delight. The last time my skin was tight, it was stretched over nine pounds of baby. Now it was just a jumble of skin with a dent in the center that passed for a belly button on a good day. I pulled the cotton blanket close and settled into the sofa, contemplating the years of cupcakes and corn chips between me and the easy elasticity of the swimsuit models.

As I clicked through the images, each more playful and carefree than the last, my daughter snuggled up to me. She noticed my screen and asked, all innocence and light, "Aren't you going to get a bikini?"

*Aren't you going to get a bikini?*

127

*Aren't you going to brush your teeth today?*
*Aren't you going to take me to school?*
*Aren't you going to make dinner?*
*Duh, Mom. It's what you do.*

At 12, my daughter was already taller than I was. And while my midriff might have a promising career as a "before" model for plastic surgeons pushing a "Mommy Makeover," my baby girl was fashion-model thin. Again, because she was 12. Her flat stomach is a mystery to me. I have never had one of those—not before my babies, not when I exercised six days a week, not when I was her age, and especially not now.

I have tried to model a healthy body image for my daughter. I cook real food, exercise semi-regularly, and try not to let her see me dissecting every perceived flaw in the mirror. I am not going to get a tummy tuck. Even though every bit of collagen in my body seems to be conspiring against me, I am only a moderate consumer of cosmetic procedures.

"I'm getting old for a bikini, don't you think?"

February is the softest month, the time of year my fat jeans are the only ones that fit. I blame it on my metabolism, which is unfair. The truth is that every year I convince myself that December's excesses did not count. In January, while others start fitness boot camps and couch-to-5k programs, I continue to gorge myself on Chardonnay, water crackers, and Havarti. Once February's reality hits and I actually start working out, my results are limited due to my aversion to "leaving it all" on the gym floor.

But there was my daughter looking at me. "Listen, Mom, only confident people wear bikinis." She was so earnest. So confident. So maternal.

Six months ago, when the slightest curves appeared on her stick-person frame, I could not force my gaze away. My obsession was part amazement for the thing I had helped to create, part delight at the wonders awaiting her, and part fear for what her physical development meant in a world that treats girls like meat and domestic service.

"Mom, you can do it. You just have to rock it."

She was right, naturally. How you carry yourself is half of any battle, and it's what on the inside that matters, and yada yada yada. But more importantly, when did she learn all that? And when had she become so good at mothering? Was this some kind of cosmic mother-daughter circle of life where everything I'd been trying to pour into her formative years came right back out and directed at me in precisely the moment I needed it?

No way.

If I believed that, I'd have to let go of my insecurities about the quality of my mothering. No one is that confident. I may or may not wear a bikini again in this life, but if I do, I'll do my best to rock it.

# Cleaning the Playroom

WE WERE MOVING. It was painful, and not just because of the boxes and the arguments over precisely the right moment to pack the living room lamps. While packing the playroom, I found the sole remainder of the Whore Barbie. Believe me when I say I'm not sentimental. As I packed, most of the toys we had been holding onto, for no reason other than that it was easier to shove them in a drawer than give them a proper burial, ended in one of many plastic trash bags. But a few things I could not throw away.

I kept the Fisher Price Little People pieces that I once encouraged my daughter to love and that she did not love. But maybe her daughter will. So I saved the best of them in a plastic tub that I imagined I'd unpack in a few weeks at the new house, tuck into a closet under the eaves, and pull out again in another life, after my husband installs gates at the top and bottom of the stairs to protect the baby who carries our DNA and toddles around our home far less frequently than we'd like.

Same with the tea set.

And the other tea set.

A long time ago, I kept a few of my son's baby clothes, including the green fleece from Old Navy that inspired me to call him my little green pepper. (I'm sorry, son, but you really have no business reading this.) I found the bag in the hall closet and packed it away—again.

My husband found the train set that no child of ours embraced, the one we searched for last Christmas so that we could set it up around the tree.

"Did we get rid of that?"

"Surely not. We would have kept that, right?"

Neatly boxed and stashed in the attic. We had no idea we were so organized.

I was not particular about how the kids kept the upstairs, except when catching a glimpse of the playroom on a particularly bad day. Piles of plastic body parts, mounds of crumpled papers, and every DVD with an annoying sound-track ever made, all seemingly multiplying before my eyes until I'd threaten to end the whole of it with an extra-large Hefty bag.

"You made me cry," my son said as we took down the curtains I sewed a million years ago.

Then we argued about the merits of a good mother. He made the case I could be nicer. I countered that nice is not a maternal characteristic worth cultivating.

I could not bear to part with the circuit kit and Erector set and an expensive system for building robotics. My husband could not let go of the broken model airplane he built out of parchment and balsa while our 5-year-old son refused to feign interest.

All the mess—packed, tossed, or just remembered—told a story of childhood well played.

Finally, amid the errant Monopoly money and 627 markers, was this miniature plastic boot from a slightly inappropriate doll my mother sent in 2008. The Girl was 8 years old then, still collecting stuffed animals and fitting on my lap. And only occasionally playing with make-believe hookers.

The new house has a family room and a living room and a media room that may or may not be outfitted by the time our imaginary grandchild comes to visit. But there is no playroom in the new house.

No playroom.

I am not sentimental, but I am holding on to the tiny boot.

# PART 3

# Farewell, Yoga Pants

❦

BEFORE HAVING CHILDREN, I thought I'd take a standard maternity leave and get back to work, but my little bundle of regurgitated breast milk had disrupted my carefully laid plans. So, after several months of early morning commutes, lunchtime feedings gone awry, and too many nights eating Hamburger Helper, I said goodbye to my beautifully neat cubicle to pursue the happiness of "stay-home" motherhood. I tried to enjoy meal planning and playgroups. I cleaned house with drive and precision. For a time, in early 2001, I even attempted a scrapbook. But instead of finding fulfillment in the domestic arts, for fifteen years I ended up working, one way or another.

Then, in May of 2013, a friend invited me to meet with executives from a little company that was doing big things in Arkansas. They needed someone who knew the online content business, and they needed her yesterday. Suddenly I faced an opportunity to join a fast-moving startup. So I slipped out of my yoga pants and into something I thought was just the right mix of corporate, casual, and cool, and which I hoped didn't look like I was really trying. I interviewed, got excited, and interviewed again. I really, really, really wanted the job.

And then I didn't get the call, which was profoundly disappointing. I stayed cranky about it for at least a month. However, the experience showed me just how ready I was for change. The fact that I had been so excited to work with a lot of other people again, for a big common goal, and the disappointment I experienced when it didn't work out felt significant. And then there was my daughter. I wanted her to see all her options, and know that it was okay to follow her ambition. I wanted to set an example for her so that in case she wanted to be a working mom, she would know it was possible. Plus, I realized I really wanted to be back in the game. It was time to get back to work in a real office with real pants.

To that end, I took on meatier consulting work and spent too much time on LinkedIn and Monster. Three months after my fruitless interviews, I got the call before the call. In a Chicago hotel room, riding high from my biggest TV appearance to date on *Good Morning, Chicago,* I congratulated the friend who had brought me in to interview. She was leaving for a better opportunity—and soon. I didn't pick up on the consequences of her move until she spelled it out.

"You know they're going to call you, right?" she said.

Two days later, from a cabin in Branson, Missouri, with spotty Wi-Fi and a strong sense that my life was going to be forever altered, I negotiated a salary and agreed on a start date only a week away.

Cue the panic.

Although I had in fact often worn pants, I hadn't actually worked in an office since 2007. I had for the most part been home for my kids. In one corner of my vivid imagination, my new life starred me as a camera-ready executive, striking deals in stilettos, and as a calm mother and wife who accomplished domestic duties on a carefully calibrated schedule. In the flipside fantasy, I was a weeping lump on the kitchen floor after learning that my children had turned into Molly-popping twerkers in their two-hour window of newfound freedom each afternoon.

To prepare for either of these inevitabilities, I embarked on an OCD-worthy cleaning binge so that I could hire a housekeeper. (You can't let them see how dirty you *really* are.) I drafted meal plans and worked out carpool arrangements. Most importantly, my husband and I had a Very Serious Talk about how our new family circumstances would play out. All the little details I had taken care of for so many years—signing the kids up for soccer, taking them to the dentist midday, cleaning up after the dog—all this would have to be split between the two of us. And frankly, during the first year in a new job, I wasn't going to have a lot of free time. The burden was going to fall on him more often than not. We planned the best we could, which is to say I made a bunch of spreadsheets. After a manicure and a trip to Ann Taylor Loft, I took myself and my Wonder Woman coffee cup to the office.

The first few weeks of work brought predictable worries.

*Should the dog stay in the house or spend the day in the yard?*

*And how was she coping emotionally with the sudden loss of her daily companion?*

*Did the kids make it home from school safely?*

*Do they have homework? And will they do it if I'm not there to remind them?*

*Are they eating enough? (And are they scoring Molly?)*

*Is my husband really okay with his new and expanded familial responsibilities?*

*Will I ever have time to see my girlfriends again?*

*When will I find time to write?*

*Or drink wine?*

Never mind that I wouldn't have time to get a haircut until Thanksgiving. Add to this my actual work responsibilities and I started to understand why half the people I know are medicated. In a panic-stricken moment, as I obsessed aloud over carpool, wardrobe, and when I'd be able paint my toes, my daughter provided much needed perspective.

"Mom, it's not like you're the first person to ever have a job."

She had a point. Almost all of my friends have demanding jobs. Half of them are mothers.

Besides, I had a superhero coffee mug. I could do this thing.

The new job proved to be as exciting and challenging as I'd hoped. After about a month, life at home had settled into a steady rhythm that, while new and somewhat awkward, was manageable and sustainable. I didn't have as much time to write, to hit my yoga mat, to see my friends. But I got more efficient with the time I did have. I paid more attention to my children when we were in the same room, took more walks with my husband, and found a new normal that was scary at times but ultimately rewarding.

I was back in the game.

If only someone hadn't gone and lost the rules.

# How Parents Work

❦

FRIENDS WITHOUT CHILDREN often remark that it's good they're not parents. "I would have no idea how to raise a child," they say.

The truth all parents know is that none of us have any idea how to raise a child, much less more than one. We cobble together an instruction manual of sorts made up of other parents' advice, pop culture, and our own upbringing, without any way of knowing in advance what kind of human will result from the particular parenting techniques we employ. All the while, we've got to convince the children we've got things under control. It's the only way to trick them into believing there's any kind of safety and structure in the world.

We do our best while comparing ourselves to other parents who don't have any idea what they're doing, either. Some parents bake cupcakes from scratch and plan elaborate parties for every conceivable celebration. Others teach their children critical life skills such as how to get into college on a full athletic scholarship. Some spend hours involved in their children's school and social activities. Some are strict and some are lenient. Despite how passionate we might be about our child-rearing ways, we are clueless until we stumble upon something that actually works. For me, there's only one thing that works for sure: tucking them into bed at night.

As my children have grown older, the ritual has become less for them and more for me. I am acutely aware that my babies will soon be gone, away at college, starting lives of their own. The thought of their inevitable departure hits me in chest while in line at the grocery store, makes me cry at stoplights, and has become part of my running internal commentary about all the ways I've fallen short in preparing them for the world at large. I never expected to become one of those moms, empty nest averse and weepy at my children's healthy human development. But here I am, worrying and indulging feelings of abandonment and sadness years in advance.

Tucking in my teenagers is one of the few times I can really talk to them for a few minutes without interruption from electronic distractions or domestic grievances. Within this small window I am allowed to hug my daughter without complaint that I'll mess up her hair. My son is not embarrassed when I kiss him goodnight. By the time my kids are ready for bed, I've given up my own nagging, having let go my hopeless dream that people put their own dirty dishes into the dishwasher. If I am very, very lucky, one of my children might offer some morsel of connection that our daylight relationship won't allow. It was in one of these sacred moments I found out my husband and I had learned something about parenting after all.

It happened while I was sitting on the edge of my son's bed, scooching the almost-too-small comforter around the hard muscles that had long ago replaced the soft little boy arms. His once-smooth skin had a faint trace of stubble, and the red bumps and dark splotches of the acne that he had been battling for months. Since first appearing, I had noticed the severity of the condition seemed to be stress-related, and it had gotten worse in the past week.

"Is anything bothering you?"

"Not really."

"Not school?"

"No."

"Friends?"

"No."

"Personal stuff?"

In response to that I received a quarter of a smile, but not even a one-word answer.

"What about Michelle?"

Naturally, I didn't expect much of an answer. He had been seeing a fellow ninth-grader for about six weeks, during which they had been to the movies, to a dance, and "hung out" at her house and ours. When they weren't together in person, they did what kids do; they maintained a continuous digital conversation.

"I guess that's kinda stressful," he said. I restrained myself from a full line of questioning, because as inept as we sometimes feel as parents, we must maintain the façade that we know what we're doing.

After a few moments of strategic silence, he let it all out. He explained the requirements Michelle had placed on their relationship, including sitting with her and her friends at lunch, answering all texts in a timely manner, and considering her feelings in his decisions about everything from where to study to what academic clubs to join. Even all that was not enough. Despite the significant time and attention Michelle consumed, she wanted more.

"She said I need to push you guys to let me go out more."

More movies, more meals, and more time alone together—as a couple. Ninth grade, ladies and gentlemen, ninth grade.

"She told me I don't fight with you guys enough."

This is the kind of moment when parents fantasize about having a handbook filled with answers.

*Had we been too strict?*

*Not strict enough?*

*Had we managed to imprint the importance of hard work and good health?*

*Were we driving him toward worthy goals or just driving him too damn hard?*

*Was it unreasonable to make him stay home when other kids were going to parties?*

*Had our limits become too constricting?*

*Where was that fine line between keeping him safe and disciplined, and becoming so rigid that he would have no choice but to follow any sweet siren's call to rebel?*

I pretended, as we parents do, that I knew what I was doing. "Well, Sweetie, when Michelle said you needed to fight with us, what did you say?"

He shrugged. "I just said… that's not how they work."

Maybe I cried a little, because I could barely contain the pure joy that wanted to explode into the space between us. I wanted to hug him and kiss him and pat myself on the back at the same time. We had done at least this one fundamental thing right. My son knew that his parents would not cave to his pressure. He knew that he was not in charge, and at least for a little while longer, didn't have to be in charge. He was safe.

*Kid, we've got this.*

For a little while longer, anyway.

And for a few more nights, I get to tuck him in.

Because that *is* how we work.

# Choose: Your Face or Your Ass

⁂

"IT'S YOUR FACE OR YOUR ASS, Honey," a wise woman once told me.

She was talking about the simple choice a woman has to make, at a certain age, about whether she wants to look good coming or going. When we're young we get to look good in the face *and* the ass, but as we accumulate years, one or the other has got to go. Deborah definitely knew what she was talking about. I've thought about her a lot this past year, and not just because I find myself torn between a good yoga-pant day and a good cheekbone day. Deborah and I graduated from the University of Washington together in 1997. We studied the same texts, passed the same exams, attended the same recruiting events, received the same honors, and finally accepted offers from the same type of prestigious firms. We were similar in every way, except that when I met Deborah in Balmer Hall, she was already forty years old.

"Is it weird?" I asked her a few months after graduation, once we had each settled into our new cubicles and lunch routines. "Does it bother you to be so much... older?"

I was not entirely thoughtful, but I was not entirely unkind either. I just really wanted to know. At 27 I was sensitive about being older than most of my fellow junior staff—by a whole three or four years. I wanted to know what it felt like to be fifteen years older than everyone else. Deborah claimed the age gap didn't bother her, but I had a hard time picturing myself at her age, working side by side with a bunch of recent grads.

Fast forward fifteen years and I found myself in exactly that situation. I wasn't sure I wanted a job, but the stars seemed to align in a role that combined my business background and my writing experience, all wrapped up in a tech startup. I'd missed my moment in Seattle all those years ago, running off to Texas and diapers while my classmates and colleagues pursued exciting careers at companies funded by the Microsoft millionaires. Now I had gone and become the oldest person in my department. My boss was technically young enough to be my son—but only if I'd made really bad choices my freshman year in high school.

When we graduated, Deborah had spent the equivalent of two months' salary on a professional wardrobe. What I wouldn't have given for the simplicity of suits and pumps. I thought of Deborah as I desperately tried to put together a wardrobe that didn't scream middle-aged mom in my new work environment, where graphic tees and flip-flops were the norm. It's not easy to convey polish and authority without looking stuffy when the manager next to you is wearing a crocheted beanie.

Not that it mattered much what I wore. I couldn't expect

to have the carefree style of a 22-year-old. I'd never have face *and* ass again. I thought of Deborah whenever I felt squishy, like after eating the single serving microwavable molten lava chocolate cake I keep on the top shelf of the pantry for emergencies. I'm not fat; I'm just not firm. When I'm bothered by my softness, I remember Deborah's wisdom and I wonder if the time has come—the time to choose. While I may not love the look of the comfort that has settled into my midsection, I have to acknowledge that my face looks fine—better than fine. Gone are the lines I noticed when I was running fifteen miles a week and I had the ass to prove it. Perhaps all the white wine and the extra baskets of chips at the Mexican restaurant serve me well. Cholesterol levels notwithstanding, gradually, an acceptance has settled in. Maybe it started when the pain after a run lasted until the next run. Or when my trick rib wouldn't stay put no matter how carefully I executed the reverse trikonasana. Maybe it was simply a realization that no matter how many crunches I did, the skin on my stomach would never smooth without surgery—and I'm not risking my life to make something look good that only my husband, my dog, and maybe an unlucky paramedic will ever see. Eventually the collagen in my face will melt away, just as the muscle tone in my ass already has. I realized my 70-year-old self would tell me to shut the hell up and enjoy my face while I still can.

This might have been the moment of clarity. What I had chased with all the diets and workouts was not health or fitness or even the bikini body promised by so many torturous boot camp commandoes, but Youth, and she runs a hell of a lot faster than I do. She does not enjoy the second basket of chips and salsa. She says no to the sweet margarita. She misses the beauty of the path because she is too busy counting the seconds until she can slow her running pace to a walk for a brief interval of peace before pushing her limits again. She does not appreciate how young and fit she is, because she is too busy working toward bathing suit model standards. She ignores the fact that even actual swimsuit models do not meet the standards of swimsuit models; their images are Photoshopped into "perfection."

Deborah showed me what it looked like to go after what you wanted, no matter your age, insecurity be damned. And surely she must have battled at least some uncertainty, with insensitive coeds asking about her age and such. She modeled grace and wisdom for me, and I'm sure every other young woman she came into contact with. Back in the workplace with all these kids, what kind of role model would I be? As the older, wiser woman, would I be the kind younger women looked up to, dispensing valuable counsel and comforting words? Or would I be the woman obsessed with my appearance—face and ass alike?

It really is time to choose.

I choose face.

So pass me a basket of chips and pour me a margarita. I raise my glass to Deborah.

# Watching

❦

I WATCHED THE SKY, hoping for a violent outburst of wind and rain. A wall cloud was probably too much to hope for. A few well-placed strikes of lightning would have been more than enough, but a tornado warning would seal the deal for sure. The coach had promised to email if practice was cancelled. So far, despite checking my inbox every six minutes since noon, the message had not come. Coach had to be watching the sky, too, possibly wondering how he'd been convinced to take the role so many years ago that had turned into a permanent position. But someone had to teach our girls, and not just anyone, but a fully vetted upstanding parent. This wasn't the '70s, when our parents paid a small fee that helped cover the cost of a coach to run soccer practice right after school (the ideal timing for keeping kids out of trouble). They didn't question the coaches' backgrounds or the reasons they might be available in the middle of the workday in that simpler time. Today's kids are better protected. God forbid someone other than a verified responsible adult show them how to dribble and pass.

Being a working mother has its moments, especially on days when I absolutely, positively cannot walk out the office door at 5:05 pm, days when our CEO complains that he is the only one in the company with a "sense of urgency." Never mind that I'd been in the office since 7:30 that morning, and spent 11 hours in my office yesterday before going home to work some more. Never mind that my team had just achieved a major win. The CEO and his MacBook were conveniently parked in a deceptively casual seating area outside my office, his vast stores of urgency presumably motivating him to be highly productive, or he was shopping for golf clubs. Either way, this was not the day to leave on time.

The closer it got to 5pm, the tighter the knot at the top of my gut. If this weather didn't develop quickly, my daughter was going to miss practice. The stress is different now than when the kids were little. Preschool pick-up times were non-negotiable. I had to be at the right place at the right time. But soccer practice wasn't *that* big of a deal, right? Not like a game. How much practice did she really need? How much could you prepare for the unpredictability of a game anyway? When I could not convince myself that missing practice was in fact okay, I did what all seasoned mothers do. I shifted the blame onto my daughter.

"You need to put these things on the calendar," I said. "We have to work these things out in advance."

*Because if it's not on my spreadsheet...*

And then, my last resort, "It really should have been your dad taking you tonight."

Your dad. My husband. Him. That man who does not

understand all I do for you, all I did before the new job and the CEO with urgent needs.

*Why couldn't it just start storming already?*

I had been calling and texting my husband all day. Just after 5:00 I tried again. No answer. I texted. I called again, and again. No answer. Then I called my daughter.

"Keep calling and texting until he answers," I told her. "I'll get out of here as soon as I can."

Getting kids to soccer practice used to be a breeze, along with doctor's appointments, oil changes, and the running of dozens of other errands that don't seem like much until you try to get them done on Saturday morning or during the thirty minutes that pass for lunch in between meetings and really important stuff I do all day on my computer. But somehow these things get done. Rather, the important things get done. I had a decision to make. Get home, knowing that practice would probably be cancelled anyway, or stay to garner more—what? Face time? Is that still a thing? There's no crying in Corporate America, and there aren't any gold stars, either.

So I drove through a developing thunderstorm to get my daughter to soccer practice on time. I pulled into our driveway, opened the garage door and honked. Then I checked my phone to find four text messages from the office, and one from coach. Practice was cancelled.

Finally.

I could finish my work from home, and now I knew what I needed to win the working mom game: just a weather machine.

# We're Puzzle People Now

❦

My kids found a puzzle in the closet. During one of their all too frequent snow days, they completed a two-sided 500-piece homage to Star Wars in the shape of Darth Vader's helmet. The puzzle was beautiful, and not just for its artistic rendering of good and evil and multicolored lightsabers. It transformed the character of my children's day. During their puzzle making frenzy they voluntarily eschewed screens of all kinds. No TV, Kindle, phone, or Nintendo received attention. For a few blissful hours, brother and sister existed for each other and a retro pop-culture jigsaw.

"We're puzzle people now," my daughter said, enfolding my husband and me into their newfound hobby.

As a family, we embraced the wholesome pastime and soon realized we lacked critical resources, ie. puzzles. A quick assessment revealed that the Star Wars puzzle had indeed been the most difficult in our possession. The kids begged me to take them to Barnes & Noble, where they could spend the remaining balances on gift cards of birthdays and Christmases past on a new conquest. We braved the snow and ice to find we had the puzzle aisle all to ourselves. I helped choose a 3,000-piece wonder of undersea life. Oh, the fishes, the coral, the barely visible sunken ship. This would keep them busy for days—weeks maybe—if the snow situation demanded. They had to have the puzzle-roller-upper-thingy, and not because they had to have it, but because I had to have it. This puzzle was a commitment, not something to be attempted and abandoned at will. The puzzle saver would help us advance through the ranks of puzzle people. I gladly swiped my credit card to cover the shortfall between my children's gift card balances and the hefty total of the puzzle and puzzle-roller-upper-thingy. Money well spent, considering the amount of sibling bonding and media abstinence it bought.

At home, we emptied the puzzle pieces onto the kitchen table and started immediately finding the edges and flipping 3,000 tiny cardboard shapes. The work was relaxing, meditative even. I savored my children's focused intensity on the task, which reminded me of simpler times—and simpler puzzles—before screens absorbed all their disposable hours and before college brochures littered their bedroom floors. Satisfied with our day's progress, and giddy from the news that the next day had already been declared a snow day, we left the puzzle on the kitchen table.

My husband was skeptical about the puzzle-making in general, and the puzzle-making in the kitchen specifically.

"We'll never eat on this table again," he said.

"Not true," I said, feeling smug. "I bought the puzzle-roller-upper-thingy."

His expression did not change.

"But we're not using it."

"We're not using it *today*," I said, "because tomorrow is a snow day."

"We'll never eat on this table again."

Day Two brought significant progress around the edges, and a good amount of conflict around the proper puzzle making technique. My son worked one corner, placing a lot of pieces in a small area, while my daughter wanted a communal effort to turn over each of the 3,000 pieces before attempting to put any of them together. Puzzle philosophy debates are never pretty, but this one turned personal.

"I'm not just going to flip over all these pieces so you can do all the glory work," she said. "You have to help flip."

She had a point.

"I'm making the puzzle," said my son, confused because he was, indeed, making the puzzle, and wasn't that the reason we were all gathered around the table?

He had a point.

Tempers rose. Accusations flew. My husband and I labored along, trying to appease both sides of the puzzle divide, but the discord ran deep. Soon, we all abandoned the puzzle, leaving it to languish on the kitchen table. I would not admit defeat—to the puzzle or my husband's pessimism about our ability to eat at the table again one day.

On Day Three we endeavored to put the past behind us and indeed started strong. Angelfish and seahorses took shape. However, just before dinner we found the dog chewing on something blue. Upon inspection we found that yes, at least one puzzle piece was lost forever. What if she'd eaten more? We had no way of knowing. At least, not until we put the thing together. Any of us could have let the puzzle piece fall to the floor. No one was confessing. The air was thick with blame. My son was heartsick. He had desperately wanted to frame the final product, showcasing our victory over complicated shapes and impossibly similar hues. In the midst of his pain, he had a brilliant idea.

"I bet we can order the missing pieces from the company!"

He consulted the box to find the manufacturer and then searched the Internet for its policy on replacement pieces. The rest of us looked at him and then each other. While we were—forgive me—puzzled by his behavior, he was resolute and growing irritated that the puzzle company did not publish a replacement policy on their website.

"Sweetie," I said. "Even if they did sell individual pieces, how would you know which one to order?"

He offered several theories about how one might identify, to a company half a world away, precisely the piece that had been mistaken for a doggie treat, but in the end had to accept the cruel truth that the fine German puzzle maker offered no solution for the problem of misplaced pieces. Moods deteriorated, the fighting resumed, this time about who got to work on the fish and who had to do the sky, which was actually just more water. We soon spent the last of our puzzle enthusiasm. It was time for our puzzle day to end. Because school had been called back into session for the next day, I decided to finally deploy the puzzle-roller-upper-thingy. Many arguments ensued and my children ordered me not to move the puzzle because they just knew that the puzzle-roller-upper-thingy would not work. Could not work.

"But it's German engineering," I said. "It has to work."

After they went to bed, and after I tucked them in, and after they told me they were still mad at me for letting the dog eat their puzzle pieces, I enlisted my husband's help to move the puzzle. I said a prayer to the puzzle gods as we rolled the puzzle and its felt pad around an inflated plastic tube. Surely, this would not work. But I was tired of looking at the puzzle. I was tired of the reef and the seaweed. Three days was enough. We had to eat at the table someday. And, good intentions aside, I had to accept that we might not be puzzle people after all. We carefully transported our giant puzzle taquito to another table, where I said yet another silent prayer to Saint Jigsaw. If I broke this thing now I'd have to find my children a new mother—one who respected the sanctity of the puzzle and bent to the will of all-knowing teenagers. Slowly, carefully, we unrolled the puzzle-roller-upper-thingy and there was the puzzle, just as it had been before—all the put-together pieces and all the loose pieces just as they had been in the kitchen. It was nothing short of a snow day miracle. The puzzle sat mostly untouched for a few more days before I rolled it up again, confident this time that our work would be preserved until we were ready to return.

That was almost a year ago.

I'm not sure when or if we'll be puzzle people again, but there's something quaint about working all those pieces of cardboard into a whole. There are worse ways to spend a snow day, and worse things to watch kids fight over. Who knows—maybe someday we'll actually finish the thing. If so we're definitely moving on: 5,000 pieces or bust. If we could finish that, we could do anything.

# Good Cop, Bad Cop

♾

MY SON IS GOING TO COLLEGE in two years. So I'm hugging him longer and pushing him harder. My husband and I discuss his strengths and weaknesses. We try to figure out ways to set him up for success, knowing that our efforts will only go so far. The majority of what he's got to do in the next couple of years, he's got to do on his own. I know it's irrational, but some days feel like my last chance to give him the best start at life.

This morning he forgot his notebook for English class. Again. It's the second time he's forgotten the notebook and the third issue with this particular assignment. First, he was confused about what kind of scrapbook was allowed. The fact that he is required to make a scrapbook for English class is another issue altogether. Why does my 15-year-old need cropping skills to get an A in English? Who knows, but he does. So we went to Hobby Lobby and bought all the supplies. Twice, actually. Because he doesn't listen very well when the teacher gives instructions.

Zander told me he had forgotten the notebook at home

just as we pulled into the Starbucks parking lot to wait for the bus. I made him call his dad to see if he could bring the book to us.

It's probably fair to say that if our family were an episode of Law & Order, I'd be the one in the interrogation room figuratively battering the perp and my husband would be cool and calm behind the glass.

"He said he's halfway to work," Zander said.

This time Dad was mad, and Zander knew he was in trouble.

"Tell him I'll take you," I said instead.

So we drove back home and had just pulled into the driveway when Zander's phone rang.

It was my husband, now more mad. He had apparently misunderstood the meaning of 'Mom will take me' and was now sitting in the Starbucks parking lot, scrapbook in hand wondering, "Where the hell are you guys?"

Whether or not Zander comes by his poor listening skills honestly is up for debate.

I'm the bad cop more than I'd like, but this time, I was the good cop. I was the calm parent, maintaining the balance. In that moment, seeing Zander so upset in the passenger seat next to me, he was my baby in the car seat—crying at every stoplight as I drove down Seattle's First Avenue in the rain while I sang and reached around to find his binky. My little boy needed someone who was okay with him just as he was in that moment, mistakes and all. That morning, I got to be that someone.

I don't know how to be a mom. I don't know how to

balance supporting my husband's parenting and comforting my baby, who is not a baby anymore. I don't know when I turned into the good cop. All I know is that day my son needed a hug. And I was there.

# You Won't Believe the Amazing Thing That Happens Next

☙

WHEN A COLLEAGUE OF MINE was recently asked what she does for a living, she said, "Whatever wakes up the CEO in the middle of the night."

She was right. That guy does not get nearly enough sleep, and he's always trying to "10x" something or other.

"You might think I'm crazy," he wrote to me in an email, "but I'm going to test something that I'm pretty sure will break the Internet."

I didn't want to break anything right then. What I wanted to do was clear my inbox, which I was doing on my phone from the lobby of the massage place where I had a standing appointment. (Some ladies have hair and nails. I've got deep tissue work.) The CEO had been pinging me all afternoon about the "revolutionary" things he was learning from a fellow high-growth tech founder. While I was certainly on board with 10X-ing anything that drove revenue, my tenure in public accounting had imbued me with healthy dose of professional skepticism. Also, I had been on this end of his exciting promises before. Part of me wanted to believe our founder knew what he was talking about, everywhere and all the time. Another part was lodged in reality. Still another part didn't understand why any of what we did actually worked. Bottom line: I didn't expect this latest plan to amount to much.

After trying without success to click through to the link the CEO had sent me—which included the words "laughing," "horse," and "noises"—I wrote him back saying I was pretty sure whatever he was about to do was probably off-brand and possibly damaging to everything I and my team had sweated to create in the past six months, but go for it. It was his company, after all. It was also 7:30 on a Wednesday night and I was about to get kneaded like a loaf of sourdough.

"Please don't break the Internet tonight, though," I wrote. "We all have a lot of work to do tomorrow."

*Post your laughing horse noise thingy. Break the damn web. See if I care.*

And care I did not. Not for ninety blissful minutes.

When I got out of my massage, I immediately indulged my bad habit. Reaching for my phone I saw a screen full of missed calls and text messages.

*Was I drunk?*

*Had our site been hacked?*

*What in the hell was going on?*

Apparently, our CEO had posted the grainiest, tackiest, lowest common denominator clickbait video compilation of animal noises the webz had ever seen. Not that I could make that statement with certainty, because I could not bring myself to watch the video all the way through. (Once you've seen 10 seconds of pig snorts and walrus honks, you've seen all three minutes.) What the video had to do with our main business (selling cowboy boots), I did not know. How it could possibly relate to the fledgling entertainment site we had built, I could not tell you. It was embarrassing at best, brand destruction at worst. But in addition to the insipid content and awful editing of Old MacDonald's Farm 2.0, there was something going on I could not deny: The damn thing was working. Our audience of boot-loving, horse-riding country music fans were going nuts for this video. Traffic was up by a factor of—you know what's coming, right?—ten.

My inbox soon filled with congratulations. Everyone who didn't think I was high thought I was a website traffic messiah, delivering visitors in unprecedented numbers. The next morning I taped a sign on my office door that read simply, "I didn't do it."

Later that day, a VP asked, "Why don't we just *make* viral videos?"

I was incredulous.

*Did he not understand our limited resources?*

*Who had time and people to produce videos?*

*You can't just* make *something go viral.*

*Virality is not a strategy!*

"Lela," he said, "I was kidding."

But our unlikely success was no joke. Over the next few weeks we posted every animal noise video ever uploaded to YouTube. My team's visibility and contribution to the business 10x'd. We adjusted to our new normal. "You Won't

Believe the Amazing Thing That Happens Next!" became a go-to component of our headlines.

Suddenly, everyone loved us and everyone wanted us to sprinkle our magic dust on their work. Worst of all, everyone sent us their favorite videos. Even my husband started sending me links to "hilarious" videos that appeared in his Facebook feed. Sadly, I knew the plot of each by looking at the thumbnail image alone. We had seen dancing Korean babies and dogs on waterslides. We had seen people jumping off buildings and babies who sing. We had seen children afraid of their father's freshly shaven faces, and mothers who fed their babies lemons only to record the reaction. We had seen bunnies frolicking in the snow and a deer crashing a family pool party. Some days we felt we had seen the whole of the Internet, which begged the question, what were we doing with our lives?

During the peak of the video posting frenzy, some other man said without a hint of irony, in his best influential tone, "How would you feel about making our *own* viral videos?"

*Wait—joking or not joking?*

I still couldn't tell, and I couldn't trust my own judgment.

What I really wanted to do was get back to publishing the things my team had grown to love—musings on the essential ingredients of sweet tea, the ideal contents of Southern girls' handbags, and polls that pitted Tim McGraw and Luke Bryan in a heated contest for 'Hottest Man in Country Music.' But there was no denying that, amid the silly videos, almost as if by magic, more people saw our real content. The asinine videos had served us well, and all our lives had been charmed by the glow of a big idea. Life was good—especially when we finally ceased pushing weird animal noises to our millions of fans.

Dreamers think bigger than the rest of us. We need them and their crazy ideas. We need their unreasonable enthusiasm for things that don't make sense until they do. I've learned to accept the insanity, to roll with it and do my best to serve it. Because big thinking, it turns out, does not adhere to logic. No risk, no reward and all that. Most important, I've come to appreciate that mad ideas in the middle of the night are some of the very best kind.

Amazing, indeed.

# Botox is a Business Asset

☙

I HOPE WE CAN ALL AGREE that Botox is insane. The fact that we are, collectively, culturally, paying others to inject poison into our faces—effectively disabling certain muscle groups that one would assume are there for a reason—is not rational. Botox is supposed to make us look younger. And we believe it. According to the American Society of Plastic Surgeons 2012 statistical analysis of American vanity (or something like that), more than six million Botox procedures were performed in 2012. It's true that some of us need a tiny bit of help, sometimes from a tiny needle. And while the importance of looking good cannot be overstated, there are other, more practical reasons to use the wonder injection.

I have a friend who likes to say—and I agree with her—that Botox can save marriages. If he can't see that face you're making, because you can't make it, he still thinks you still think he's fantastic. And we all know more than one marriage that has not survived a man's sudden knowledge that his wife doesn't think he's fantastic all the time. Or half the time. Or twenty-percent.

Up your odds! Shoot up your face. It worked in Stepford; it can work for you, too.

If marital bliss doesn't inspire you to calculate how many units it will take to disable your visible irritation lines and start filling up your Botox punch cards, think of the business advantages!

We all work with idiots, right? I don't care how much you love your job. I don't care how connected you feel to your colleagues. I don't care how high a road you aspire to take. I guarantee there are some morons working beside you. Or, if you're like me, dozens of them—but they're only temporary morons, which is to say that they're smart people who suddenly become stupid when they don't agree with me. How great would it be to simply look upon these poor unfortunates among us without a hint of expression? With zero physical manifestation of judgment? Surely, a person who could master this trick would soon win ALL the friends and influence ALL the people.

I'm onto something here. If you have a speck of gray matter inside that skull, you'll agree. If not, that's okay. You won't see the scorn hidden beneath these immobile facial muscles.

I almost forgot the best part: Guys can do it, too! Finally, a business advantage that's not just for the ladies. So next time you're wondering how to get ahead at work, forget acquiring new skills or buttering up the boss. All you need is Botox.

For love, for money, for life.

You're welcome.

# Slumber Party

❦

"HOW ABOUT A SCAVENGER HUNT?" I asked my daughter as we got into the car to pick up party supplies for her fourteenth birthday.

She gave me that look. The one all mothers of teenage girls know—the expression that says you—of all the humans on Earth—you are by far the most pathetic, irrelevant, hopelessly ignorant imbecile who ever had the poor judgment to breathe the same oxygen as your teenage daughter.

"Oh. My. God, Mom! That is so fourth grade. Everyone will think it's totally lame."

The scavenger hunt idea might have been a reach, but the party was starting in a few hours and so far all we had were Cheetos and cake. We needed a plan to diffuse the inevitable social tension that I knew was coming. It was inevitable considering the guest list, a mix of my daughter's new and old friends. At the big public middle school, Gaby had been part of the elite—athletes and cheerleaders, kids who shop in stores that reek of AXE and entitlement. They were the quintessential popular girls destined for the ruling class as eighth grade upperclassmen. But the previous fall, Gaby had changed to a small college preparatory charter school that rewarded a different type of achievement. Faculty and scholars alike lavished special treatment on Quiz Bowl champions and science fair competitors. The basketball team had played for three years before winning their first game. Gaby adjusted to her new world quickly, not only to the uniforms and rigorous academics, but also to a smaller group of friends, and their more refined interests. My daughter did not give up her loves of nail polish and soccer, but her life became richer with new friends who could make a pun quicker than they could quote a Katy Perry lyric.

During the school year, Gaby managed to split her time between the old and new friends. This party was her first attempt to unite the two groups. Everything needed to be just right. Once upon a time I knew how to throw a party that made her happy. We had a ladybug party when she turned two. The next year, we threw a fairytale ball—complete with a princess cake that had a real Barbie sticking out of a decoratively frosted cake gown. (Pre-Pinterest, thank you very much). We had a blast doing facials at her fourth grade spa party, and the next year, when we made tie-dyed shirts. But this time I was useless. Gaby had rejected every one of my ideas. No ice cream sundae bar, no cooking class, no friendship bracelet arts and craft night. She was turning 14. Her friends were practically grown women. We had to entertain them accordingly.

"Are you sure you don't want to do a scavenger hunt?" I asked again as we set up the big beverage server with enough raspberry lemonade for the entire cheer squad and debate teams combined.

"No, Mom! That's, like, for babies. Do you want everyone to think I'm a baby?"

"I'm pretty sure a baby couldn't do a scavenger hunt," I said.

Sarcasm as a parenting tool produces varying results, but at least it makes me feel better.

"Just never mind, okay? We're just going to hang out."

When Gaby started sixth grade at the big public school, I became The Mom Who Knows About Mean Girls, asking her too often about her social life and how she was treated and how she treated others.

"I don't know what kind of middle school you went to, but my school isn't like that," she told me once. "It's not like people are *all mean and stuff*."

But she's wrong. Because everyone knows middle school is hell. That is a universal truth for all times. Those years are especially heinous for girls, who are genetically predisposed to being *all mean and stuff*. Clearly, my daughter had been spared becoming a target, but sometimes I worried she was on her way to becoming one of the Mean Girls herself. And while I'm pretty sure my girl wasn't personally mean, I'm not sure she was sticking up for anyone either. I'm not proud of equating popular with mean, but I've been there. I know these girls. Sometimes they can't help themselves.

Mean or not, Gaby's old friends were worldly in a way that her new friends were not. And vice versa. Make no mistake, nerdy chic girls had skills. Each of them knew which constitutional amendments had granted their favorite rights, as well as how to properly place a semicolon. They will undoubtedly grow into women who govern our nation and cure our diseases. Still, these girls are unaccustomed to the ways of The Squad. And we were about to bring these very different girls face to face. My daughter wouldn't admit it, but I suspected she was just as nervous as I was.

Thirty minutes later in our backyard, the girls assessed each other with judging glances. They took turns laughing at very different kinds of jokes and consulting their phones more than necessary. Gaby was visibly tense. I lurked, watching the group's body language through the kitchen window. In a stroke of brilliance I pulled out the conversation starter cards we sometimes used during dinner and called Gaby into the house.

"Yes?" I said, holding up the plastic cube that held a hundred ice-breakers.

I got the crazy eyebrow. Then the eye-roll.

"No, Mom! Jeez."

Out of the sight and earshot of her friends I reassured her that I had her back.

"If it gets bad and you change your mind, just tell them your lame mom made you do it."

This is my standard instruction to get her out of any situation, from refusing a date to escaping party where there is sure to be trouble. Blame it on me, any time.

"Okay," she said, and humored me with half a smile.

After dinner the girls reverted to their "hanging out"

state, and migrated to Gaby's room. Their interactions had become by turns painfully quiet and increasingly awkward. I knew because I listened at the door. That is, until my husband pulled me away.

"They're fine," he said, fooled that the sound of laughter meant the girls were getting along.

He had no idea. The subtext of teenage girl laughter is a whole other language. I on the other hand knew too much, and was busy projecting my own middle school terrors onto these girls. I still wanted to be the hands-off mom when it came to my kids' social lives, but the stakes were too high. Without exaggeration, this was the most important sleepover of Gaby's life. I felt responsible to do anything I could to make it a success. This was all new territory for me, trying to engineer the inner workings of my daughter's friendships.

A little after eight, Gaby came downstairs with a request from the group.

"They want to know if you can take us to the mall."

Where, presumably, the girls would continue to "hang out."

I was ready to grab the car keys when my husband gave me a look, his look. He was right. The mall was a terrible idea. I tried to be bright when I suggested for the 235th time, "How about a scavenger hunt?"

*Why couldn't I let it go?*

"Mom, I told you, no one wants to do that!" She retreated again only to emerge two minutes later.

"I have been proven wrong," she said. "They actually want to do a scavenger hunt."

*Yes!*

I made a quick list and then tried to play it cool while I told them my only condition: I make the teams. Surprisingly, they agreed without argument and I quickly broke up the two groups into two new groups. Girls from different worlds would now have to mix. And mix they did, for over an hour, running around in the dark giggling like—well, like little girls. After hours of uncomfortable interaction they found common ground looking for sticks and taking pictures with cats. They found the neighborhood drainage ditch and that sign at the edge of the empty lot that says either Private Property or No Trespassing, and then they debated about what it actually said.

And then they really hung out, all of them together as one group. It would never happen again, but that wasn't important.

When it was all over, after the movies and the snacks and the French toast breakfast casserole, and all the girls had rolled up their sleeping bags and rolled away in their parents' cars—after all that, I got that look: The one that said I wasn't so bad after all.

# There's No Crying
## in Corporate America 2.0

❦

SHERYL SANDBERG TOLD US IN *Lean In* that she had cried at work. She said a few tears didn't mean you were weak, but I didn't believe her. Besides, I work with men. And here's a thing about men: They tend to freak out when they see a woman cry. And even if they don't "freak out" per se, they don't quite know what to do with feminine emotion. So if you want to get ahead in a male-dominated corporate culture, it stands to reason you want to keep your weeping on the low. Cursing and slamming your hand on the table, however, is probably acceptable. But crying on the clock? Not cool.

When I decided to go back to work, I didn't return to something I knew. I didn't find a position where I could take it easy, bust out my ten-key and destroy some 1040s. Instead, I thrust myself into a completely foreign, extremely challenging, super-chaotic startup, where I was hired to launch a business unit that was not just new to the company, but just plain new—as in no one on the planet knew how to do the job I'd be given. I had a vague idea of a direction of what might, maybe, sort of, could work. The company had no clue. Naturally, we were all fairly optimistic.

For months my job was really, really, really hard. Everything felt like a fight. When I wasn't fighting, I was drowning. Fighting is not easy when you've just caught your breath. One particularly bad day, after months of my work and planning were literally handed over to a snot-nosed MBA, I lost it. I spent the entire day walking around the office red-eyed and pathetic, afraid to go into the bathroom because I might see myself the mirror and lose it for real. I felt like everything I'd been drowning and fighting for had been taken away, which made me want to bang on some desks. In fact, that probably would have been healthier. But, like a good girl, I held everything in until it was safe to cry, which I did for an hour after work, into the phone to the friend who had gotten me the job.

A few months later, a young woman I'd worked with on a few projects asked to speak to me. She closed my office door and told me about a dispute she was having over her annual review and compensation. She was upset, and got so angry while she was telling me the story that she started to cry.

I listened. Then I gave her some advice that I hoped with every hoping cell in my body was right. Two hours later I received a text thanking me for staying late, for listening, and mostly for my advice, which had worked.

I had helped. Good as that feeling was, I was selfish too. Building this woman up meant there would be one more woman who would grow to advocate for the rest of us, and maybe give me wise counsel the next time I was on the verge of tears, like the day I started to lose it in front of the woman I work most closely with every day.

"Are you okay?"

"I'm fine."

"Seriously, what's going on?"

"Stop being nice to me. You're going to make me cry."

"Seriously, who do we have to go beat up?"

I got her to leave my office and watched her tell another woman to come take care of me. When the other woman came into my office, she was shaking her head.

"I told her it's just hormones."

A few months later, two of us walked in on another woman having a moment, and naturally, we were nice, so naturally that caused her to cry. She was spilled all her frustration and all her anger, at one of those ridiculous dramas that happen in every workplace. If the year had taught me anything it was to trust my instincts. So I just went up and gave her a huge hug, the squeezy kind that attempts to wrestle out all the bad feelings.

"They're assholes," I told her over and over without knowing who or what had upset her.

It seemed I spent the entire year in tears. I'd never been so emotional at work, which was evidence of just how much and how rapidly I was growing. It wasn't pretty, but it was a necessary burning away—or melting—of the old me, the old ideas I had about what it was to be a strong woman. One day I broke down in the bathroom, unable to hold it together.

"I'm sorry, this is so stupid," I managed to say to the

woman in there with me. "I'm sorry. Just don't pay attention to me."

"It's okay," she said. "I'm just happy to see you're like… a real woman."

Just like that, she put me at ease. I didn't have to have superpowers every day. Strong women are all around me, and I want to be like each of them.

I want to be the woman who listens, no matter how hysterical the rant.

I want to be the woman who is strong enough to ask for help.

I want to be the woman who will fight for a friend.

I want to be the woman who knows better than to pick a fight.

I want to be the woman who lets it all go.

I want to be the woman who can comfort with few words.

I'm starting to wonder if Sheryl might be right. Maybe crying is okay.

So long as you never do it in front of a boy.

# Playing Pretend

☞

UNTIL THAT DAY WE DECIDED to make a baby, I hadn't spent much time thinking about life with kids. I just assumed we'd have them, eventually, because that's what you did. Kids were part of a life that fit within the lines, which was all I ever wanted. It's the reason I became a CPA and married an engineer who excelled at table manners. All my earliest memories revolved around playing house. I spent long, rainy days behind our farmhouse in Northwest Washington collecting eggs, picnicking in the shade of an ancient apple tree, and watering the nettles behind the garage as if they were my own garden, just like the one my parents grew. I chopped bright green blades of grass, making believe they were onions for a salad I'd serve to imaginary friends. I rolled and shaped homemade Play Doh while my mother worked the real stuff into loaves of white bread, which we finished with butter, sugar, and cinnamon before it had time to cool. I played house beside my young mother doing the same. After my parents divorced, I started playing school and office, too, but I kept playing house indoors or out among hundred-year-old evergreens.

Once I started growing an actual human and preparing for his birth, I wasn't so sure I could handle it. I worried that I wouldn't know how to be a parent, that my upbringing had not provided me the skills to nurture a family. As much as I liked to play house as a child, I never dreamed about the white dress or the two-point-five kids. In middle school, my friends and I consulted the Ouija board about boys who would be our future husbands, who were all named Curt or Travis or Kyle, but when it was my turn, the fortune telling speller stayed put. Every time I twisted the stem off an apple, reciting the alphabet to ascertain the first initial of my future True Love Forever, I landed on Q. As for children, I didn't care for them. Like other teenage girls, I babysat, but only for the cash and, at certain houses, the Atari. I did not particularly care for any of the children that I knew, so making my own hardly seemed logical. Besides, I was going to be busy in a glamorous occupation, such as cruise ship activity director, supermodel, or someone who fought crime while maintaining exceptionally feathered hair. I might have settled for grocery checker or bank teller, but not Wife. Not Mom.

It is possible I inherited my lack of domestic ambition from my mother, who wore sequins to my school choir concerts long before they were appropriate for daytime wear. In her defense, they were part of her stage wardrobe. My mother fronted a series of Top-40 cover bands. Throughout my formative years, a parade of Paul McCartney and Rick Ocasek wannabes filed in and out of the basement. They arrived and departed in various states of sobriety, and with varying levels of enthusiasm for playing "Hit Me With Your schedules of three other humans, medicate a dog, match socks, and make a mean pie crust. I also lead a team at one of the fastest growing ecommerce companies in the country. I select tasteful paint colors and set a proper table. I plan, coach, and clear my inbox. Occasionally I wear an apron, sometimes with heels on. I fight for my projects at work, and make it home for dinner most nights. I turned out to be a pretty good wife and mother.

I have absolutely no idea what I'm doing.

Let's keep that between us.

ACKNOWLEDGEMENTS


WORKING WITH SMART and talented people is truly a gift that never stops giving. I have been blessed to know and work with more than my fair share of such people. For that I am truly grateful.

Thank you Adrienne Crezo, for being just the right mix of friend, therapist, and editor. Thanks for enjoying the occasional spot of "rapper gin," and for knowing every common and obscure grammar rule, because you actually enjoy them. Thank you for helping transform a collection of essays into a single story. Your guidance about endings will be with me for the rest of my writing life.

Thanks to Nancy Cleary for never-ending patience, and for making it all so easy.

To all my former colleagues at Arthur Andersen, thank you for unending support, and for the pumping room, which was certainly before its time. Thanks to every one of you who also had a baby in 1998, so that our cubicles became a pre-Internet fount of infant care wisdom, or at least speculation.

Thank you to every manager, director, editor, and client throughout the years who has welcomed me onto the team. Thanks for teaching me the lessons and skills I call on every day. To everyone at Country Outfitter, but especially the Media & Entertainment team—Lauren Cowling, Kelli Lott, TJ McDaniel, and Christina Stumbaugh—thank you for making our office a place I want to spend my days.

Thanks to Michelle Cove, Christa Hines, Rhonda Franz, Ellie Grossman, Cindy Hudson, Malia Jacobson, Christina Katz, Lara Krupicka, Heidi Luedtke, Judy Miller, Hollee Schwartz Temple, Bridgid Schulte for your early support, kind words, priceless input, and for being some of the very best role models I could ever hope to know.

Thanks to the friends who continue to support my writing and who shamelessly promote my books and suffer my borderline-pathologic social media activity. Thank you Angie Albright, Lori Bremer, Kristin Frei, Lyndi Fultz, Sarah Hood, Amy James, Shannon Magsam, Stephanie McCratic, Jennifer Quezada, Gwen Rockwood, Lori Walker, Tina Winham, and Gracie Ziegler.

Thanks to Diana Calhoun, who is conspicuously absent from these stories. I thank you for listening to most of these before they made it to the keyboard, and for giving me the best advice when I am feeling especially off-balance.

Thanks to my parents, Lou Nicksic and Marilyn Levan, and to my extra parents, Jacquline Nicksic, Alexander Davidson, and Elvira Davidson, who all help me keep my balance and pick me up when I fall down.

Thanks most of all to my husband, John, for supporting everything I've ever wanted to do.

And to the children, Gaby and Zander—you're welcome. Everything chronicled here has been for you, and always will be.

Lela Davidson is VP of Media & Entertainment at Acumen Brands and the author of two award-winning books, *Blacklisted from the PTA* and *Who Peed on My Yoga Mat?* She speaks nationally about motherhood, marriage, marketing, and media. Her work as a freelance journalist and essayist has appeared on Today, NBC News, and NPR.

www.leladavidson.com